KING ALFRED'S ENGLISH

A History of the Language We Speak

and Why We Should Be Glad We Do

Laurie J. White

King Alfred's English

Library of Congress Control Number: 2007902186

ISBN 978-0-9801877-1-7

The Shorter Word Press
1345 Butler Bridge Road
Covington, GA 30016-4935

www.theshorterword.com

Cover image by Comer Turley, Turley Photography LLC

Norway

Sweden

Scotland

Hadrian's
Wall

NORTH
SEA

Denmark

Ireland

WALES

England
Britain

Thames River

Cornwall

London

Channel

English

Original Homeland
of the Angles, Saxons,
and Jutes

ATLANTIC

Normandy

Brittany

*Paris

Germany
Germania

OCEAN

France
Gaul

The Alps

Pyranees Mts.

Spain

Italy

To
Rome

MEDITERRANEAN
SEA

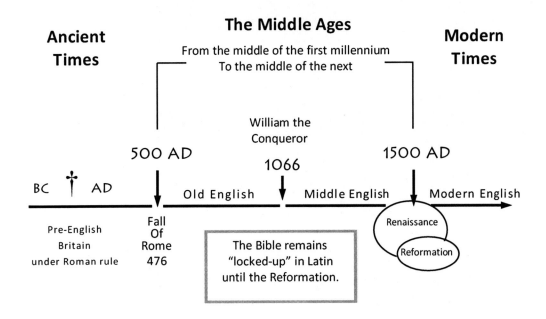

The Middle Ages
From the middle of the first millennium
To the middle of the next

Ancient Times

Modern Times

William the
Conqueror

500 AD

1066

1500 AD

BC ✝ AD   Old English   Middle English   Modern English

Fall
Of
Rome
476

Pre-English
Britain
under Roman rule

Renaissance

Reformation

The Bible remains
"locked-up" in Latin
until the Reformation.

Old English

Invasion of
Latin
& Old Norse

- c. 500 AD—King Arthur (if he really lived)
- 731—Bede finished his Ecclesiastical History of the English People
- c. 800—Beowulf written
- 871—Alfred became king of Wessex
- 1016—King Cnut won the throne of England

Middle English

Invasion of
French

- 1066—William conquered England; French became the official language of the English court
- 1382—Wycliffe's Bible (handwritten) began circulating in England
- 1400—Chaucer died with The Canterbury Tales unfinished
- 1456—Gutenberg's Printing Press
- 1476—Caxton's printing press—1st in England

Modern English

Invasion of
Greek
plus more Latin

- 1526—Tyndale published the first English NT in print; executed for heresy 1536
- 1611—King James Bible published
- 1616—William Shakespeare died

Free supplemental material for students is available at www.theshorterword.com

- Chapter Worksheets
- Unit Tests
- Links to related online literature and primary sources
- Links to articles, images, and videos that expand the topics in each chapter
- Suggested movies

In memory of my mother, Frances Napier Jones,
who loved books, poems, grammar and, most of all, Alfred.

Acknowledgments

I'd like to thank Dr. Frederick Montesor, a former college professor of mine. I took his History of the English Language course back in 1972 at Auburn University. Dr. Montesor's enthusiasm and knowledge gave me a lasting love for the subject of how English developed. Thirty years later, I still had all of my notes and handouts from his class and was able to use them as a reference and guide to help me research this book. My emphasis on the "language law" comes straight from him.

Thank you to Fran and Bob Lewis, my promoters and encouragers, who gave the chapters their first proofing as I churned them out. They prodded me to keep after it and their corrections and suggestions were thoughtful and vital, helping me cut through random ideas and stay on track. Marika Mullen was invaluable as she gave the manuscript more professional editing. Also, I appreciate Sue Jakes, author and editor for Great Commission Publications, taking the time to read my manuscript. Her enthusiasm for the project was such an encouragement that I kept her initial phone message on my answering machine for two years so I could replay it whenever I hit a slump. Finally, thank you, Anne Dicks! You rescued me on the final lap and, in the midst of your own busy schedule, gave the book a final proofing.

I'm grateful to Roger Walshe at the British Library for his help and through whom I received permission to use their website's activity pages in my online supplemental material. The library's website is user friendly with quality lessons for students and it was a continual resource for me.

Finally, thanks to Rebecca, Hetty and Robert Lee for being my guinea-pig students and for being interested in this material long before it was in a book.

Table of Contents

Your Native Tongue

What does it mean to say a particular language is your "native tongue"? Perhaps, more than you think. Did you know that in recent years it was discovered that if you learn a language before the age of puberty, you learn it in an altogether different part of your brain? Also, researchers have found that unless you learn a language as a child, and in this other mental compartment, you will probably never speak it without an accent.

The language you learn as a small child is the language of your heart. It is the one in which you call out when you are hurt, the one in which you holler when you lose your temper, the one in which you pray.

Is English your native language? If it is, then what we are about to study is the language of *your* heart and the wonderful and sometimes very surprising ways by which it grew to be the crafty, agile, skillful, undaunted, cardio-kleptic language that we speak!

Crafty < **Old English**
Agile < **Latin**
Skillful < **Old Norse**
Undaunted < **Old French**
Cardio-kleptic (heart-stealing) **< Greek**

Part I

Pre-English Britain

55 BC – 500 AD

Have you ever wondered why England has two names? It is sometimes called Britain and sometimes England. Of course, it is also called the "UK" for the United Kingdom, but that came about in modern times. The names Britain and England are much older.

However, at the very first of our story, England was not yet called England either. In ancient times it was just called Britain and no one had even heard of England or the English language. In fact, when Julius Caesar came to Britain in the century before the birth of Christ, Britain was just a primitive land on the outskirts of nowhere. It was inhabited by wild and warring clans of people who, a few centuries later, would end up doing their very best to prevent the English language from ever coming to the shores of their island home. They were highly unsuccessful.

When Togas and Latin Came to Britannia

Chapter 1

Veni, Vidi, Vici.

"I came, I saw, I conquered."
Julius Caesar

Caesar Conquers Gaul and Britannia

In 55 BC Julius Caesar landed in what we know as England today. He called it Britannia, the land of a people known as the Britons. He had just finished his conquest of Gaul, the old Roman name for France. Both the Gauls and the Britons were part of a much larger group known as the Celts (pronounced *Kelts* or *Selts*, either way).

There are some very definite characteristics that make historians lump these people together into one group. The first is their languages. From studying the grammar and vocabulary used by these Britons and Gauls, linguists can tell their languages were close kin and from a common base. They also had the same religion for the most part, that is, the Druidic religion. Druids were a special class of men among the Celtic people. They were the rulers, the leaders in warfare, and also the priests. They led the people in the worship of many gods and a strong belief in the afterlife. They thought oak trees and mistletoe were sacred and held most of their religious rites and sacrifices in oak forests. Our custom of kissing under the mistletoe at Christmas time is a cute twist on some old Druid beliefs.

Other areas around Britain besides Gaul were also Celtic at this time. Look at the map just inside the cover of this book. Find Wales. It is part of the same island as Britain but is separated from the rest of Britain by mountains. Now look at Ireland, which is separated, obviously, by the Irish Sea. Then there's Scotland, the top part of Britain. Like Wales, Scotland is separated from the rest of the island by rough, mountainous terrain. Last of all, in the south is little Cornwall. By now you can guess: there's another mountain range separating Cornwall from the rest of Britain. Whenever you see distinct differences in culture between areas that are close together on a map, you can bet there is some geographical feature that separates the two, something hard to cross like a wide desert or a rugged mountain range. In 55 BC, Celtic people inhabited all of these places—that is, Gaul (France), Britain, Wales, Ireland, Scotland, and Cornwall. (Notice that *England* did not yet exist.) All these areas had their own dialects, tribes, and chiefs, but all were Celts. There was another group of Celts who had settled in Asia Minor, our present-day Turkey. Their Celtic language was Gallic for they were related to the Celts in Gaul. The apostle Paul wrote them a letter and it is part of our New Testament: the book of Galatians (*Gaul*-atians).

After conquering Gaul, Julius Caesar sailed across the English Channel to conquer Britannia just to say he could. Caesar didn't like thinking that anyone was above Roman rule. Britain was of no real use to the Romans at that time, and the Romans didn't really intend to settle there. They hated the climate. It was rainy and chilly, and though it was never terribly cold, it was never terribly warm there either. So Caesar built some temporary fortifications and left a few troops there, but only for a short while.

Then, around a hundred years later in 43 AD, Emperor Claudius I decided that Rome should go back to Britain, re-conquer it, and this time establish some permanent forts and buildings and convince a few Romans to actually settle there.

Fighting Druids

The Celtic people in Britain were fierce fighters, but they didn't stand much of a chance against the Roman Empire's advanced weapons and war tactics. The Romans had catapults and a cavalry, and, to top it off, the Romans even had their own version of a tank—elephants. You can imagine what the average Briton thought of these huge, strange beasts. He'd never even heard of an elephant, let alone seen one. The Romans floated them over the rough waters of the

English Channel and terrorized the Britons with them. But more importantly, the Roman army was a highly organized and trained war-machine, unlike the Britons who were only temporarily banded together to fight a common enemy. Britons, as a matter of fact, usually spent a great deal of time fighting each other.

However, the Romans had to fight much longer and harder than they had anticipated because these Celtic Britons did have two distinct factors on their side. First, they were absolutely fearless warriors. They fought at times with such total abandon that they sent waves of terror through the ranks of even the battle-hardened soldiers of Rome. They sometimes dyed their faces blue, as did the Celtic Scots in the movie *Braveheart*, and gave out fearsome, bloodcurdling battle cries as they charged. (Some historians think their battle cry may have been the fore-runner to the famous rebel yell of the Southern soldier during the American Civil War). Along with the blue faces and the hollering came loud blasts from a multitude of blaring war-trumpets made of rams' horns. The whole effect was pretty overwhelming.

Second, their women often fought alongside the men and were even scarier! The wives of the Druid priests reportedly fought with a vicious frenzy unlike anything the Romans had ever seen. Tacitus, a Roman historian, described an attack by Druid warriors: "On the shore stood the opposing army with its dense array of armed warriors, while between the ranks dashed women in black attire like the Furies, with hair disheveled, waving brands." Another Roman author, Marcellinus, described a Celtic woman fighting "with flashing eyes, she...begins to rain blows mingled with kicks like shots discharged by the twisted cords of a catapult." There was a Celtic queen of this era named Boudicca. When her husband was killed by Roman soldiers, she led her people in several amazingly successful battles against the Roman army, but was then finally defeated. Our word *bodacious*, meaning outlandishly bold, comes from her name. Bodacious sounds like a good adjective for Celtic women in general.

In the end, the ferocity of the Celtic warriors could not defeat the immense and efficient army of the Roman Empire. Claudius eventually won, and Britain came under Roman rule. After victory was more or less secured, the Romans began setting up a few forts that eventually became towns. The most important of these was Londinium Fort. It, of course, turned into London, the capital city of present-day England. London is located on the Thames River (not pronounced as it is spelled—say *Tĕmz*). The Thames became a kind of liquid highway for travel and trade in England.

Some of the Celts in the northern regions, especially the Picts and Scots, were harder to subdue. They kept on attacking Roman outposts until Rome gave up on trying to control these rowdy hordes. Finally, after a century or so of fighting off these early Scottish highlanders, the Roman Emperor Hadrian built a rock wall to mark the northern boundary of Roman rule. The wall was eight feet thick, 20 feet high, and 80 miles long. It kept the un-subdued Celts separate from the subdued Celts. Most of the wall still stands there today. It is known as Hadrian's Wall (see map).

The Romans founded several towns: Bath, Canterbury, Caerphilly (in present-day Wales), as well as London, to name a few. With buildings as high as four and five stories, tiled roofs, beautiful mosaic tile floors, plumbing, and even central heat in the nicer homes, these towns flourished. Picture a bustling town brim full of educated nobility, servants, slaves, and a solid middle class all speaking Latin and wearing togas...in England! And it lasted almost 400 years.

Many Roman ruins can still be seen in England today. The city of Bath, known for having the only hot springs in England, has some of the best-preserved Roman buildings and baths. Roman roads can still be seen in many places as well. In fact, Rome was famous for her roads. There was nothing like them anywhere else in the world. Paved with stones, extending miles and miles crisscrossing a vast empire, they made the traveling easier for certain evangelistic apostles of the first century AD to take the good news of a Savior to all parts of the world. The Roman Empire persecuted Christians off and on for nearly three centuries, but despite being fed to lions in the Coliseum and other Roman cruelties, the Christians endured, and their faith spread like a brush fire. Throughout history, the winds of persecution have always made the fire of the gospel burn brighter, and those wonderful Roman roads literally paved the way for the sparks to spread.

Constantine

In the fourth century AD, a man named Constantine was fighting in a civil war over the throne of the Roman Empire. One day he had a vision. There are several variations to the story, but basically he claimed that he saw the "sign of the Christ" in the sky and a voice telling him he would win if he fought under that sign. With renewed hope, he had the first two letters of the word Christ in Greek, *chi* (X) and *roe* (P), put on the standards of his army. He won the battle and converted to Christianity. Constantine became Rome's first Christian emperor and he made Christianity legal all over the empire. Finally, the persecution of Christians by the Roman Empire was ended.

The Chi-Rho symbol for Christ is always depicted with the *Chi* placed over the *Rho* as Constantine presumably saw in his vision. The symbol has been used by the church throughout history and is still popular today in religious artwork from stained glass windows to

352 AD Roman coin showing the Chi Rho symbol on the back. Used with permission. www.cngcoins.com

altar cloths. Occasionally at Christmas time, you might see someone use the abbreviation *Xmas* for Christmas. This shorthand for Christmas is not sacrilegious as some people think. It is not x-ing out Christ, but rather using the traditional Greek initial *Chi* to stand for the first letter of Christ in Greek, just the way Constantine did.

By the time of Constantine's conversion, there were already groups of Christians in England among both the Romans and the Britons who lived there, and now that the emperor himself was a Christian, they could openly worship the Savior without fear of persecution. The new faith spread and many more people were baptized. As history testifies, this newly adopted religion of Rome would prove to be even more durable than its stone-cobbled roads.

The Gospel in a Shamrock

It was during this new Christian era of Rome's occupation that a certain sixteen-year-old boy in Britain was kidnapped by a raiding party from Ireland. The Irish were still a pagan people and made a habit of pirating the coastal lands nearby whenever they felt like it. The boy's name was Patrick. His captors took him back to Ireland where they sold him as a slave to a farmer. He endured long, hard months of labor under a harsh owner who didn't understand a word of Patrick's language.

Though Patrick's parents were Christians, Patrick himself had never thought too much about religion and had not committed his life to Christ. Now, he had plenty of time to think about God while he slept out in the cold watching the farmer's sheep, and, with his situation both desperate and miserable, it wasn't long before he sought to be reconciled to the only One who could help. He surrendered his life to God. As Patrick wrote later in his *Confessio*, "[God] guarded me, and comforted me, as would a Father his son." Then one night he heard a voice saying to him, "See, your ship is ready." Patrick believed it was God telling him to escape. So, he risked the harsh punishment that awaited him if he were re-captured and headed for the coast. A ship bound for France "just happened" to be docked right where Patrick ended up, and the captain was willing to take him aboard if he helped with the work. He arrived in France and made his way to a monastery. He stayed and studied under the monks for a while but eventually was able to travel back home to Britain. He would have liked nothing better than to just stay there, but God had other plans.

Patrick began to sense that the Lord was calling him to take the news of the gospel to the very folk who had so brutally enslaved him. Returning to Ireland, he spent the rest of his life in a missionary effort to win the Irish tribes to Christianity. Because of the great success of his work there, we know him today as St. Patrick, and St. Patrick's Day is celebrated each year in his honor.

Irish tradition says that Patrick used the common three-leaf clover, or shamrock, to explain the concept of the Trinity to his new converts. The shamrock remains the most recognized symbol for Ireland to this day, and in the hearts of Christians everywhere it stands for God's miraculous work in and through the man named Patrick.

Rome Gets Vandal-ized

The Roman Empire started having major problems around this time—from both inside and out. Inside, it was inflation, government corruption, and a huge government debt. Outside, it was Germans. Yes, Germans, but they weren't called that yet. "Germania," the general area we know as Germany today, was full of heathen tribes like the Ostragoths, the Visigoths, and the Vandals (from which we get our words *vandal* and *vandalism*). These tribes were uncivilized and uneducated compared to the highly advanced and educated Christian Romans, and they liked the climate of Italy and France and the loot they found when they won a city. So, they started coming down into Gaul and Italy to take over one city after another. They had no centralized government, but they had a common religion and culture, and their languages had a common base which linguists group together as being *Germanic*.

As Roman cities came increasingly under attack from these northern barbarians, Rome began to bring her troops closer to home, abandoning the more distant outposts and far-off places. Britannia fit that description. So, in 410 AD the last of the Roman troops left Britain. The towns and forts were abandoned. Latin would never again be the common tongue in that part of the world. But, hey, that left the Celts free at last after having their territory occupied by foreigners for centuries. Culturally they were still distinctly Celtic, not Roman. However, they had added Christianity to their cultural soup, along with its accompaniment of well-educated monks and priests and the language of Latin, the language used by scholars for all formal books and important records.

The End of an Empire and the Close of an Age

Now, look at the timeline at the front of this book. Officially, Rome fell as an empire in 476 AD. Historians mark the end of the Roman Empire as the official close of ancient history. The next period—with which most of this book is concerned—is the Middle Ages. If you round up the date for the fall of the Roman Empire to 500 AD, then it's really easy to memorize the dates for the Middle Ages: 500 AD to 1500 AD, an even thousand years. That means the Middle Ages went from the *middle* of the first millennium to the *middle* of the next. Get it? That's why it's the *middle* ages... That's not really the reason for the name, but it will help the dates stick in your mind. So Rome fell, ancient history closed, and the Middle Ages began.

The beginning of the Middle Ages marks the beginning of the history of our language because, with the Romans gone, Britain was now vulnerable to the *next* invasion, the invasion that brought English to the shores of England.

✠✠✠ Æ ✠✠✠

AD 435.   This year the Goths sacked the city of Rome, and never
          since have the Romans reigned in Britain.

The Anglo-Saxon Chronicle

Well, We're Through with the Romans...

So Who's Next?

Chapter 2

> AD 449. King Vortigern gave [the Jutes] territory in the southeast of this land, on the condition that they fight the Picts. This they did, and had victory wherever they went.
>
> The Anglo-Saxon Chronicle

How Do You Un-Invite a Jute?

When Rome pulled out, Britain was left undefended and ungoverned. The Celtic clans had never been more than just loosely organized. Now, they were left to themselves. However, they did have one unifying element now that they had not had before: Christianity.

A British chief by the name of Vortigern was being continually bothered by those same northern tribes that Hadrian's Wall had been designed to keep out. With no Roman troops to guard the wall anymore, the Picts and Scots began coming down and plundering, looting, and ransacking many villages that were under Vortigern's rule. At this point, Vortigern made a strategic error. He called for help from a tribe of Germanic warriors across the sea known as the Jutes. With the promise of good pay, these Jutes from Germania (see map) welcomed something profitable to do, so they answered his call, boarded their ships, and sailed to Britain to push back the Picts and Scots.

The Jutes fought well and got rid of the offending tribes. Alas, however, the island looked good to them, the weather didn't trouble these Germanic folk at all, and they decided to stay and settle, not just take their pay and leave. This greatly vexed Vortigern. The Jutes turned on the Britons and began fighting them for their villages and lands. Then two other Germanic tribes got the idea from the Jutes and started moving in too. The Jutes, you may have never heard of, but these other two you probably have: the Angles and the Saxons. Today, historians refer to all three of these tribes jointly as the *Anglo-Saxons*.

So, just when the Britons had the island all to themselves at last, they were invaded again. And, unlike the Romans, the Anglo-Saxons didn't want to rule the Celtic people, they wanted them to leave, vamoose, scram, vacate the premises. The Britons were killed, enslaved, or driven out of their homeland, and as they went, Christianity was driven out with them. These conquering Germanic tribes were all pagans who called on Thor for help, along with a whole slew of other gods and goddesses.

The majority of Britons fled west to Wales. Wales is still part of the same island, but it is separated and protected, as mentioned earlier, by mountains. Such a large number of Britons sought refuge in Wales that the invading Anglo-Saxons often referred to the fleeing Britons as "the Welsh," because that is where they ended up. These Christian-Celtic-Britons fled to other areas as well. Basically, this is where they went (look at the map to see where these areas are located):

West: to Wales and the more southern country called Cornwall.
        Also, they fled even farther west across the Irish Sea to Ire-
        land. Ireland was more civilized now since St. Patrick had
        helped Christianize it.
North: to Scotland to join those wild Picts and Scots (who were
        Celts themselves, just slightly wilder ones).
South: across the English Channel to the north of France. That area
        in France is still called Brittany today for the Britons who
        settled there. Today, the people of Brittany still speak the
        language called Breton, though most everyone there today
        also speaks French, of course.

There are many Celtic languages. Here's a list of them all so you can see:
- Irish Gaelic (spoken in Ireland)
- Scottish Gaelic (Scotland)
- Manx (spoken on the Isle of Mans, a large island between England and Ireland)
- Breton (Brittany)
- Cornish (now extinct—once spoken in Cornwall)
- Welsh (Wales)

- Gaulish (now extinct—once spoken in Gaul, ancient name for France and colonies such as Galatia)

All the Celtic languages are in danger of dying out though many efforts are being made to preserve them. Gaulish has been extinct since around the 5th century, and the very last native speaker of Cornish died in 1777. Her name was Dolly Pentreath.

So, to summarize what happened, just picture Germans: Germans going south to Italy and causing the collapse of the Roman Empire; Germans (the Franks) going into France and taking over there, too; Germans going into Britain and pushing out the Celts. Just picture Germans going everywhere—conquering, marauding, pillaging, pushing out in every direction as they spread out from their own homeland. It kind of makes you wonder about the Germans, doesn't it, especially since both World War I and World War II were fought against Germans. But, of course, before you actually get down on Germans, remember, if you're of English decent, that's *you*.

King Arthur and the Knights of the Round Table

It is during this time in history that King Arthur, if he really lived, rallied a large force of Britons around him and took a stand against the invading Anglo-Saxons. So, he was Celtic, not English. Or, you could say he was British. He was *British* but not *English*. Gets a bit confusing, doesn't it?

The earliest accounts of him are in Welsh writings, which is logical considering the Britons fled to Wales. An ancient Welsh historian named Nennius around AD 770 refers to him as an actual person and hero of the Britons, calling him Artorius, a Latin rendering of his name. Nennius wrote that Arthur was part Roman in his heritage, which makes sense because the Romans did not pull out of Britain until shortly before the Anglo-Saxons began moving in. The legend of King Arthur grew gradually over the years with different elements being added at different times by Celtic bards and by the French who always have loved anyone who fought the English. Around 1138 Merlin, Guinevere, and Excalibur (Arthur's sword) made their appearance through the writings of another Welsh historian, Geoffrey of Monmouth. Less than a century later, the French added Sir Lancelot, the Knights of the Round Table and the search for the ever-elusive Holy Grail, the cup from which Christ drank at the Last Supper. Various authors throughout the Middle Ages continued to tweak the story, adding elements of their own and subtracting others, with each version offering a new slant on the old themes.

In our own time, novelists and filmmakers have reshaped the legend for modern audiences, from T. H. White's novel *The Once and Future King* (the source for Disney's animated *The Sword in the Stone*) to the more recent 2004 film *King Arthur*. Arthur may have never truly lived, but his story certainly has. Its major themes of love, betrayal, honor, and the dream of a kingdom founded on the ideals of justice and equality has drawn audiences from around the world and across many centuries.

✠✠✠ Æ ✠✠✠

AD 591. This year there was a great slaughter of Britons...

The Anglo-Saxon Chronicle

Part II

Old English

500—1066

The Middle Ages are usually broken down by historians into two parts, the early Middle Ages and the late Middle Ages. Sometimes the first half is also called the Dark Ages though scholars now feel that this period was not nearly as "dark" as once thought—lots of learning and discovery were actually taking place. The English spoken during these so-called Dark Ages is known today as Old English, but back then it wasn't old at all. It was lively and spry, and now it had a whole new island to conquer.

A Little About Language

Chapter 3

Language is the means of getting an idea
from my brain into yours without surgery.

Mark Amidon

Old English

In case you haven't caught on yet, when Britain was taken over by the Angles, Saxons and Jutes, the whole territory ended up getting its name from the Angles. It became *Angle-land*, so to speak. Actually, the Anglo-Saxons called it *Angelcynn*, which morphed into *England*. And that's how there came to be two names for this one island: Britain and England. Each name represents a different group of people who inhabited the same territory at different times.

As the first inhabitants, the Britons, got pushed out by the invading Anglo-Saxons, their language got pushed out with them. Sometimes place names linger on after a big invasion. Consider how many places in America have Native American names. From the states (Oklahoma, Delaware) to the rivers (Chattahoochee, Oconee), from the mountains (Appalachian) to the deserts (Mojave), Native American names are everywhere! But it was not so with the Anglo-Saxon invasion. These Angle-ish renamed practically everything. All the old Roman names for roads and towns, as well as the ancient British names for villages and hills, rivers and valleys were changed. The place names that did linger were mainly those that end in *chester* or *caster* (that's an ending that comes from the Latin word for *camp*). Thus, places such as Gloucester and Winchester are all old Roman encampments which became towns. Also, some towns such as

London and a few other early forts kept their former names as well, but, for the most part, it was a complete wipeout.

The Anglo-Saxon people spoke what they called *Englisc*. Scholars today call it Anglo-Saxon English, or just simply Anglo-Saxon. It is also commonly referred to as Old English. You may have thought Shakespeare spoke Old English, but he didn't, at least not by linguistic standards, though it may sound very old to you and me. Actually, Shakespeare was the best-known writer of *modern* English. Old English, or Anglo-Saxon, is so different from our own speech that it is almost like a foreign language. It has to be translated or we can't understand it. Shakespeare may have some antiquated vocabulary and references we don't readily get, but if you attend one of his plays where you can see the emotions acted out with the words, you can understand everything that's going on. Well, almost everything.

But what *is* this language we call English? Where did it come from? Is it derived from some other language or did it spring up on its own? In fact, do languages ever spring up on their own, or do they all go back to, you know...the Tower of Babel? And what type of language is it, besides being Germanic, whatever that means?

The Grammar Game

First of all, let's look at how languages are put together. A language is somewhat like a card game. It consists of vocabulary and grammar. The vocabulary is the deck of cards, and the grammar is the rules for the game. The deck is useless by itself because without some rules no game is possible. And just as knowing the rules makes playing the card game possible, knowing grammar makes communication possible. Without grammar, no one could even talk.

All some at understand without basic other could rules we each not.

The unintelligible sentence above has a proper set of vocabulary (the deck of cards), but it breaks every rule of English syntax, or word order. When re-written according to the rules, the sentence reads:

We could not understand each other at all without some basic rules.

Grammar, which includes syntax, penetrates much deeper than just getting a subject and verb to agree or avoiding ending a sentence with a preposition. Grammar consists of rules we begin learning as soon as we start saying our first words. Anyone who can talk with intelligible speech has absorbed and digested grammar rules so complex that it took years to discover and describe them. The amount of grammar you already have tucked away inside your brain, whether you know it or not (and regardless of what your teacher says), is astounding!

So, we've got the deck of cards and the rules for playing, but do the rules ever change? Definitely. And how about the deck of cards? That changes, too. Let's look at how.

The Language Law

I'm going to teach you a law that governs language development. This is the number one principle that describes how languages change over time. Living languages (those that are being spoken everyday somewhere) are always changing, and they are always changing in the direction of becoming more simple, never more complex. Put more concisely:

> Living languages always simplify over time.

This language law does not mean that a language doesn't grow and add great heaps of new vocabulary and fresh phrases. English certainly has a much larger vocabulary than it did a thousand years ago. But the structure of its grammar has only done one thing: simplify. And this pattern holds true for all other languages as well.

Take Latin for example. Over the years that it was being spoken in the Roman Empire, it gradually grew less complex in its structure. There were fewer declensions of nouns, adjectives and pronouns, and simpler conjugations for verbs (don't worry if you don't know what all that means). However, once people no longer spoke in Latin, but merely wrote in it or studied it, it froze in time and no longer changed. When a language is no longer in everyday use, it is called a dead language. Latin is a dead language. So is Ancient Egyptian or Akkadian. Nobody is speaking these today, and so they are no longer changing.

But English is alive and well, and it has been changing over the centuries and is still changing today. Also, it is easy to see how English has not only changed but has simplified over time, too. For instance, take the word *you*. Today one little word serves the purpose for what we call the "second person." But if you go back to 1600 when Shakespeare was writing his plays, there were four words from which you had to pick — *thou, thee, ye,* and *you.*

Consider these simple sentences using our modern word *you*:
> **You** have stolen my apple!
> I'll have no lunch now because of **you**.
> Will **you**, my friends, help me get my apple back?
> If so, I'll share it with all of **you**.

In Shakespeare's day this would have been spoken thus:
> **Thou** hast stolen my apple!   [singular—subject]
> I'll have no lunch because of **thee**.   [singular—object]
> Will **ye**, my friends, help me get my apple back?   [plural—subject]
> If so, I'll share it with all of **you**.   [plural—object]

Notice that it is not until the very last sentence that we get to the *you* we use today. And that's not all, for the possessive form of *you* there were two more words to choose from—*thy* and *thine*, whereas today we just have the one word *your*. *Thy* was used before words beginning with a consonant, and *thine* was used before words beginning with a vowel, the exact same way we use *a* and *an* today.

The thee's and thou's were pretty—that's one reason everyone still loves the King James Version of the Bible—but aren't you glad you don't have to worry about case forms for *you*? And that is just one example. There are hundreds more. English has been greatly simplified in its grammar over the centuries leaving us only a few case changes for our pronouns (I/me, he/him, she/her, etc.). Just think, at one time you had to use a different case form for every single noun depending upon its function in the sentence.

Language—Evidence for Design

This language law actually produces an interesting conundrum. If languages only simplify over time, how did mankind develop complex languages in the first place? Language could not have developed from caveman grunts to complex linguistic structures, at least not without intentional supernatural input. However, pure evolutionary theorists insist that just such a shift must have occurred as early humanoids evolved into full humans. They have various theories as to how this might have happened but, so far, no real evidence.

In the 20th century, primitive and isolated tribes were encountered as civilization encroached on their territory or as missionaries sought them out. Evolutionists were hoping to find a tribe that exhibited a less evolved language, a tribe speaking a Stone Age language to go with their Stone Age culture. Such a discovery would have gone a long way to back up evolutionary suppositions. To their surprise, however, these primitive tribes, from cannibals in Papua New Guinea to the Motilones of western Venezuela, were discovered to have highly complex language structures, leaving evolutionists disappointed but still looking.

So what is the answer? Do languages ever spring up on their own? Do they ever evolve from the very simple to the highly complex? Christians who take a literal approach to Genesis do not believe so. They think instead that language was given to man full-blown and complex from the first moment of creation. The complexity of primitive languages and the fact that languages are observed to simplify over time are seen as clear evidence for supernatural design.

According to the Bible, God's nature is a Fellowship. He is a group within Himself—loving, laughing, singing, working, creating, and communicating. Our own ability to fellowship and bond through the use of language is a reflection of His image stamped upon us at creation. Completely taken for granted by all of us most of the time, language is an astonishingly complex medium of exchange for our ideas and thoughts. More than anything else, language is a gift, and it was given to us by the One who most desires to communicate with us.

Sir William Jones Goes to India

Though there is a great divergence of languages on earth, there are marked groupings or families of languages. English is one branch of the larger European linguistic family tree. As it turned out, that particular family had an interesting surprise in its history just waiting for a brilliant language buff to come dig it out.

In 1783 an Englishman named Sir William Jones was sent to India. He was a lawyer and a judge and had been appointed to the supreme court of Bengal, India. England, as you may know, ruled India at this time just as she had ruled the American colonies. More importantly, Jones was also a philologist. Philology is the study of ancient texts and languages and Jones was a whiz at languages. He had learned Greek, Latin, Persian and Arabic by the time he was in his early twenties. So he was excited by his new appointment to India with its ancient language, archaic texts, and exotic customs and religion. It was a whole new field to explore.

As Jones began to study Sanskrit, the ancient language of India, he made a startling realization. Sanskrit had some words in it that were similar to both Greek and Latin and, amazingly, English. Sanskrit and English? Yes. When Sir William Jones published his research in 1786, it was a ground-breaking book called *The Sanskrit Language* in which he put forth the theory that Greek, Latin, English, Persian, Sanskrit, and also the Celtic languages plus a few more, all came from an older language that no longer exists. His findings were the very first evidence brought forth for what scholars today call the Indo-European language. It is a theoretical language. No one can prove it existed. But the study of the vocabularies of all these varied languages has shown similarities that go far beyond what could ever have occurred by random chance.

There's been a lot of research since Jones's book was published, and linguists agree that the Indo-European language did exist, and they can take many words back to what probably was their original form in that language. Much is still speculation, but the common source is a pretty sure thing. All these related languages are categorized today as Indo-European languages, and the original language is usually referred to as the Proto (first) Indo-European Language, or "P.I.E."

The following chart shows words in eight different Indo-European languages so you can see the similarities for yourself. The top row shows the possible reconstructed words from the Proto Indo-European Language.

P.I.E.	nokwt	ster	snigwh	sawel or sun	mens
MODERN ENGLISH	**night**	**star**	**snow**	**sun**	**moon/month**
GERMAN	nacht	stern	schnee	sonne	mond
LATIN	noctis	stella	nivis	sol	mensis
GREEK	nuktos	aster	nipha	helios	men
RUSSIAN	noch'	------	sneg	solntse	mesjats
SANSKRIT	naktam	str-	snih- 'sticky'	surya	mas-
SPANISH	noche	estrella	nieve	sol	mes
FRENCH	nuit	etoile	neige	soleil	mois

The Brothers Grimm

Now, there are two more people I want you to know about who are wrapped up in this whole business of reconstructing the Proto Indo-European Language. Have you ever heard of the Grimm brothers? Perhaps not, but you have probably heard of Grimms' fairy tales. A majority of the well-known stories commonly called fairy tales are actually very old German folk tales written down in the 1800's by Jacob and Wilhelm Grimm. Because of their love for German history and folklore, they scoured German villages interviewing hundreds of old people and country folk who remembered the stories from their childhood. "Little Red Riding Hood," "Cinderella," "Snow White," "Hansel and Gretel," and practically every fairy tale you would consider a classic comes from their research and writing.

What most people do not know, however, is that both of these brilliant men were also philologists. Jacob Grimm in 1822 came up with what is known as Grimm's Law when he documented the fact that all the

Germanic languages (including English) had gone through a series of sound shifts that followed a definable and predictable pattern. It's all about unvoiced stops (like our *p* sound) becoming unvoiced fricatives (like our *f* sound), and voiced stops becoming something or other, and if you really want to know what all this means, there are plenty of books and Internet sites that will fill you in on every detail. Suffice it to say for our general purposes, Grimm had discovered a linguistic trail of breadcrumbs, and following it led to a breakthrough in language study. Grimm's Law demonstrated for the first time that systematic, not just random, changes had occurred in a language. Language experts were now able to trace the derivations (histories) of our English words with much greater precision, telling which came from Latin or Old French and which were direct descendants of Anglo. So, whenever you look up a word derivation for an English word, you may very likely owe the answer to the careful scholarship of Jacob and Wilhelm Grimm, and, of course, we have all these great fairy tales, too.

An Inflected Language

We have seen that Anglo-Saxon was from the Germanic branch of the Indo-European family of languages, and it had finally arrived on the shores of England. It is a living language and, as such, is always changing and always in the direction of becoming more simple. Therefore, Old English was more complex than modern English. So, let's look just a bit at how it was more complex.

One of the primary characteristics that made Old English more complex is that it was highly inflected. Inflections are changes we make to a word depending on its grammatical function in the sentence. We still use a few of these changes in modern English. For instance, we change the tense of a verb with the inflection *-ed* to make it past tense (*walk— walked*). Or we add *-ize* to some nouns to make them verbs (*modern— modernize*). You can change the adjective *cautious* into a noun by putting *-tion* on the end instead of *-tious* and you get *caution*. The simple adding of an *-s* to indicate the plural of a noun is an inflection, too. These tack-ons, or suffixes, are just one type of inflection.

Inflections also include changes to the actual root of the word, such as going from *good* to *better* to *best*, or from *mouse* to *mice*. The root word *good* morphs into a different form altogether to show comparative and superlative forms, and *mouse* mutates when it becomes plural. We have already looked at the way Shakespeare in 1600 had four words from which to choose for our one word *you*. *Thou, thee, ye, you,* are all examples of root-change inflections that Old English employed but modern English has since simplified. Inflected languages show singular/plural, gender, verb tense, etc. by tacking on suffixes or by changing the root itself. So that was English at this time in history. Almost every word had an inflection of some kind to show its function in the sentence.

However, Old English had a relatively small vocabulary compared to today, partly due to the fact that these Germanic heathens were not terribly civilized. Think about it. If you live a simple, primitive life, you don't need twenty different words for positions in the government; you just need one or two—chief, warrior. You don't need dozens of words for your kitchen equipment, furniture in the house, or different types of dress and hairstyles. Compared to the more sophisticated cultures represented by Latin or modern English, this was a stripped-down language for a stripped-down culture.

Our English vocabulary today is huge compared to what it was back then, and the words that have been added were borrowed from many different languages, as we shall see. So which words in our speech today are actually Anglo-Saxon in origin? Of the 100 most commonly used words in English today, all 100 are Anglo-Saxon. Of the next 100 most used words, 90 of them are Anglo-Saxon. These words are the essential build-ing-block words of our language, such as *here, there, the, is, you, that, when, where, way, water, night, game, god, good, a, and.* We could not speak without them. I had a college professor who liked to say that if you have two or more words in English for the same idea or object, the shorter word would usually be the Anglo-Saxon word. There are exceptions, of course, but generally speaking this is a good rule of thumb. For instance,

> *light* is AS (Anglo-Saxon) --- *illuminate* is Latin
> *keep* is AS --- *retain* is Old French
> *eat* is AS --- *ingest* and *consume* are both Latin

As you can see, the Anglo-Saxon is often the simpler, more primitive word.

More Invasions

In the centuries to follow, there were more invasions on the island of England, but the Anglo-Saxons were never driven out. They were there to stay. However, these next invasions made a great impact upon their language—our language—serving to shape it, change it, simplify it, enlarge it, and make it one of the most flexible languages in the world. It is by far the language with the largest number of words, which makes it great for creative writing...and terrible for taking the SAT. All you have to do is compare dictionaries to see the difference:

> French dictionary – 100,000 word entries
> Russian – 130,000
> German dictionary – 185,000 word entries
> Oxford English Dictionary – 615,000 word entries

The next chapters will deal with each of the language invasions in turn and show how each changed the way we speak and enlarged our vocabulary. The word *invasion* is not intended here to mean a military invasion, although two of the four were definitely military in nature. But all four were cultural invasions that shifted and shaped the English people in many ways, including their language. The invasions were:

> 1... The Church and Latin
> 2... The Vikings and Old Norse
> 3... The Normans and Old French
> 4... The Renaissance and Greek

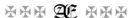

AD 671. There was a great death of birds.

(The only entry for that entire year)

The Anglo-Saxon Chronicle

The Invasion of the Church and of Latin

Chapter 4

AD 596. Pope Gregory sent Augustine to Britain, with a good many monks, who preached the gospel to the English people.

The Anglo-Saxon Chronicle

Augustine of Canterbury

We have established that the Anglo-Saxons were a pagan people and that they pushed the Christian Celts out. So England, which had received the gospel on its shores once already, needed it again. Enter Augustine. Now, this is NOT the Augustine who wrote treatises about the Christian faith, who is often quoted on theological topics, and who is referred to as one of "the early church fathers." If your pastor quotes an Augustine in a sermon, it would more than likely be this better-known Augustine, Augustine of Hippo. The Augustine of whom you're about to learn, Augustine of Canterbury, though not as famous, is more important to our study because he brought the light of the gospel to England.

Our Augustine was sent to England by Rome. By "Rome" I don't mean the Roman Empire, for it no longer existed as an empire. But the city of Rome still existed and it had retained its status as the central headquarters for the Christian church in Western Europe; that is, the Roman Catholic Church or, simply, the Catholic Church. The idea had taken root that one bishop, namely the bishop of the city of Rome, should have authority over all the other bishops in all the other Christian churches of the former Roman Empire. This one bishop was now referred to as "the pope," from the Latin word for father.

At this time, the pope was Gregory I, and he wanted Augustine to go to England to convert the heathen people there. Augustine was not too keen on this idea because he had heard terrifying reports of the savage pagans who inhabited the island. He even asked Pope Gregory for another assignment, but Gregory refused. What neither of these men knew was that God had already prepared the way for Augustine. England had been divided into seven sections belonging to the Angles, Saxons and Jutes. Each section had its own king, as well as its own dialect, too, but they all spoke Anglo-Saxon. Take a look at this map to see who settled where.

When you watch movies or read books about England, from Robin Hood to Jane Austen, you'll hear these tribal territories mentioned. All of the early chiefdoms live on in the names of the present-day shires, or counties, of England. Look at any modern map of England and you'll see *Middlesex*, *Essex*, *Sussex*, etc. And now you know why -*sex* is at the end of so many English place names—it's short for *Saxon*.

Bert and Bertha

Aethelbert, the English king of Kent, had married a woman named Bertha. Surprisingly, Bertha was a Christian, practically the only one among these pagan Anglo-Saxons. She was a princess from another Germanic tribe that had settled in France and had converted to Christianity. The kingdom of Kent also just happened to be the place your boat would probably land if you were crossing the English Channel, which, of course, Augustine was preparing to do. So when Augustine landed with his small convoy of monks, he landed in Kent (see the map). Bertha encouraged King Aethelbert to be receptive and courteous and to listen to what these Christians had to say. The king put them up in comfortable lodgings in the town of Canterbury, and not long afterwards Aethelbert gave Augustine the opportunity to explain the gospel. The king converted to Christianity and decided to make sure everyone in Kent heard the message of God's love. He was baptized on June 2, 597, and the new faith spread from Kent out to all the other Anglo-Saxon kingdoms. The English church was born.

As for Augustine, he was later appointed by the pope in Rome to become the very first Archbishop of Canterbury. The title of archbishop is a high office in the Roman Catholic Church, and, throughout the rest of English history, whoever was Archbishop of Canterbury held the highest position in the church in England.

Centuries after Augustine's death, the Roman Catholic Church declared him a saint. Declaring someone a saint is a particular custom of the Catholic Church and a practice that Protestants do not keep. However, many of the stories of the ancient saints are fascinating tales of faithful Christians living for Christ under harsh or unusual circumstances. From Saint Nicholas (the man Santa Claus is based on) to Saint Francis of Assisi, many of their stories are well worth our knowing and remembering. Many, like Saint Augustine of Canterbury, were true heroes of the faith displaying courage in taking the gospel to pagan peoples.

From Saxon Runes to Roman Alphabet

Notice that we have a date for the actual day and year of Aethelbert's baptism. That's because, along with Christianity, scholarship had now landed on the island. The coming of the church meant that for the first time historical events would be recorded in books and reliable records would be kept—reliable because they were written, and writing was something the Anglo-Saxons didn't do very often. Anglo-Saxons did have a special type of writing called *runes*, an alphabet of symbols that were sometimes carved into the handles of weapons or stone markers and inscribed on jewelry or other types of ornaments. Runes were also used for all sorts of magical spells because it was believed the markings had special powers. But only a few documents were written in runes, mainly because most Anglo-Saxons were not literate (able to read and write) and because paper was rare. Then, as Christianity spread, education and literacy spread with it. Paper and ink became available at the local monastery along with educated monks who could teach you to read and write, and so the Roman alphabet of Latin was quickly adopted. It is the one you and I use today. What you are looking at now on this page is actually the ancient Roman symbols for sounds. Even the name of the font most often used on computers, Times New Roman, hearkens back to the origins of our alphabet.

Meanwhile, because the church at this time was the prime source of education, all scholarly documents were kept in Latin, the official language of the church. English was considered "vulgar" or common (the original meaning of *vulgar*). Latin was deemed formal and scholarly. English was destined for greater things later on, but in the meantime, what a helpful boost the Latin was to English! Since everything from scientific treatises to histories, from church services to every official business of the courts and the government, was all spoken or written in Latin, a multitude of Latin words was adopted straightway into the English. Many of the religious or philosophical concepts in Latin had been unknown among the English, and many of the possessions of these more cultured people were totally unfamiliar, so it was natural to just take the new idea or object and call it by the name these educated Christians called it.

Here is just a miniscule sampling of words that English adopted from Latin at this time:

abbot	candle	elephant	psalm
altar	cleric	martyr	sponge
cancer	deacon	mass	tunic

Notice in the list above how many of these words are related to religious practices. Words related to Christian beliefs and practices of this era make up the largest percentage of the newly adopted words.

The Gast and the God Spell

Of course, many new ideas were also picked-up and then actually translated into the English, giving new meanings to Old English words. For instance, the Old English words *halig* for *holy* and *gast* for *spirit* combined to make *Halig Gast*, which evolved into the modern English *Holy Ghost. God spell* is old English for *Good News,* and as you can tell, that's where we get our word *gospel.*

You may want to know, if *god* meant *good*, (as in *god spell*), then what was Old English for *God?* It was also *god*. So, god was God, and god was good, too. Get it? No? Well, it's like in English today where we say *bank* for a slope of ground and we also say *bank* to mean a place where we deposit our money. The two words do not mean the same, yet they are both spoken and spelled the same (such words are known as *homonyms).* So, too, were the words *good* and *God* in Anglo-Saxon, and since God IS good, how fitting (and funny). An Anglo-Saxon could say, "God is god," and mean it two different ways.

Our Pagan Days

After mentioning the great quantity of Christian-based Latin words adopted into English at this time, we should also note the fact that pagan beliefs of the Anglo-Saxons linger on in our language as well. For instance, names for four of our days of the week are straight from the gods and goddesses of the Anglo-Saxons:

Tuesday—Tew or Tiu's Day, the god of war
Wednesday—Woden's Day, the god who carried off the spirits of the dead

Thursday—Thor's Day, the god of thunder

Friday—Frigg or Freya's Day, the goddess of love

The names for Sunday and Monday are the Germanic version of the Roman name for that day. In other words, the Romans called the first day of the week after the sun. It was *Dies Sol* in Latin for Day of the Sun, and the Anglo-Saxons picked up that idea but used their own word for the sun and called the day Sunday. Same thing with the moon for the second day...*Dies Lunae* in Latin became *Monday* (*moonday*) in English. Saturday, which is named after the Roman god Saturn (*Saturnus* in Latin) was the only day of the week that kept the original Latin word for its name. It's Anglicized a bit, but pretty much the same. Our days of the week are a good example of how these early English folk mixed together their Germanic heritage with the Latin-Roman culture of the newly arrived Roman Catholic Church.

Latin: An International Language for Scholars

The gleaning of Latin words during these early Anglo-Saxon days was not some one-time thing. From this point on, and for well over a thousand years, Latin was the language which all highly educated men used when they were writing their highly educated treatises. So, new Latin words just kept on coming. That's why so many of our scientific and medical terms are Latin. Latin even became an international way of communicating among scholars. If an Italian scientist wrote a paper on his study of planetary movements, he wrote it in Latin. Thus, an English or a French scientist could easily read it because they also wrote and studied in Latin. The two scientists did not need to speak each other's primary language. They both just needed to know Latin.

The Language that Became a Prison

Ironically, while Latin was offering greater freedom of communication to scholars, it became a kind of prison for the Bible. Latin was on its way out at this time, and within a few centuries it was a dead language; that is, it was no longer the everyday speech of any country or group of people. Latin had, of course, been a fully alive and functioning language during the long history of the Roman Empire and throughout this early period of the Middle Ages. However, the countries once ruled by Rome had now split off into independent states and cities, and it wasn't long before the languages of these various places began evolving into the many different Romance languages (*Romance* as in *Rome*—not flowers and a box of candy). Italian, French, Spanish, Portuguese, and Romanian, for example, are all considered Romance languages because they all come from Latin. So, in a short time, linguistically speaking, Latin was dead and no longer understood by the general, run-of-the-mill folk. The problem was that the only complete translation of the Bible that was around in all of Western Europe for over a thousand years was in Latin. After all, the only church was the *Roman* Catholic Church, and it kept Latin going post mortem out of its ties to the traditions of the early Church of Rome.

Unfortunately, all this boils down to the fact that eventually only the upper crust of society—the educated monks, priests, judges and scientists—could read the Bible because only they could read Latin. To make matters worse, the notion gradually took hold among many church officials that common, uneducated people could not possibly understand the scriptures without someone trained in theology to help them. Therefore—and this they sincerely believed—it might actually be dangerous to translate the Bible into any of the common languages.

This view was not so widespread in the earliest days of Anglo-Saxon England about which we are reading now. Books of the Bible were freely translated into common English during this period of time. When we get to King Alfred, the first king of England and the man for whom this book is named, you'll see that he was busy promoting English in all areas of learning and scholarship, including Bible translation. But with the passing of the centuries, the Church became more and more entrenched in its stance. English, especially, came to be viewed as too primitive and ordinary to express the great truths of God's Word. In church services, the priest might translate certain portions of scripture into English to use in his sermon, but most of the service as well as the scripture readings were in Latin.

You cannot understand the Reformation, which we will cover later on, if you do not fully grasp what began to happen here. The Bible at this time was just in handcuffs, but it was being slowly ushered toward a top security prison, and was eventually locked away in Latin for the rest of the Middle Ages. No one, whether in Spain, or France, or Germany, or Italy, or England, had the Word of God in his own language. In England, it even became a crime punishable by death to translate scripture into English. But that story we will leave for later.

Illuminated Manuscripts

During the Middle Ages a practice of decorating and illustrating special books developed. We know these books today as *illuminated manuscripts*. These were manuscripts of the Bible in Latin that were decorated with colorful designs. The artwork was amazingly elaborate representing hours upon hours of labor by the artist, usually a Catholic monk who lived in a monastery. Sometimes the artist drew pictures that actually went along with the text, illustrating (*illuminating*) the Bible story

Illuminated page from the
Lindesfarne Gospels c. 715

on those pages, and sometimes the designs were abstract for the sake of beauty alone. And beautiful they were! Probably the best known illuminated manuscript is the Book of Kells, a hand-copied text of the four New Testament gospels in Latin. Irish monks at a monastery in Ireland produced it around 800 AD, and it is considered one of Ireland's national treasures.

But England had its illuminated books, too. A rival to the Book of Kells is the Lindesfarne Gospels, another early text of the four gospels. Beginning around 715 AD, a monk named Eadfrith worked for six years copying and decorating the gospels in Latin. He

lived at Lindesfarne Monastery on Holy Island, a small island off the coast of Northumbria. A later monk (900 AD or so) named Aldred decided to add a translation of the gospels into Old English underneath each line of Latin. Thus, the Lindesfarne Gospels, a treasure to begin with, also became the oldest surviving text of the gospels in the English language.

The "Our Father"

One of the passages of the Bible that was often translated into English was what we know today as the Lord's Prayer. These early English people called it the "Our Father" because that's how it begins. Here it is in Anglo-Saxon with a line-by-line translation. Before you look at the modern English translation, see how many words you can recognize in the Old English.

Old English	Word for Word Translation
Fæder ure þu þe eart on heofonum,	*Father our thou that art in heavens*
Si þin nama gehalgod	*be thy name hallowed*
to becume þin rice	*come thy kingdom*
gewurþe ðin willa	*be-done thy will*
on eorðan swa swa on heofonum.	*on earth as in heavens*
urne gedæghwamlican hlaf syle us todæg	*our daily bread give us today*
and forgyf us ure gyltas	*and forgive us our sins (guilt)*
swa swa we forgyfað urum gyltendum	*as we forgive those who-have-sinned-against-us*
and ne gelæd þu us on costnunge	*and not lead thou us into temptation*
ac alys us of yfele soþlice	*but deliver us from evil truly.*

Do you see the letter that looks like a *p* but is shaped a little differently? It is the letter *thorn* [þ] which we no longer use, and it stands for the sound *th*. The [ð] symbol, known as an *eth*, also stands for our *th* sound as well. That's strange, I know—two symbols for the same sound, but they were used in slightly different ways. Another archaic symbol is the *ash* [æ] that represents the short *a* as in *cat*. King Alfred's name was originally spelled with the ash at the beginning in its capital form: Ælfred.

One other interesting aspect of Old English is that it used the letter combination *hw* instead of our modern *wh*. It looks backwards to us, for instance:

while was spelled—hwil

where—hwær

whistle—hwistlian

which—hwelc

This peculiar looking *hw* is actually the way we still pronounce the *wh* even though modern English has reversed the order of the letters. The breathy *h* comes out before the *w*, that is, if you pronounce that *h* at all. You—if you're younger than around 40 years old—probably do not voice the *h*. To test and see, say the pairs of words below. Do you pronounce these words differently or the same?

whether and weather

where and wear

If you say each pair the same way, you've dropped the sound of the *h*, and you're part of an ongoing language shift that's happening today. Try testing your parents and grandparents, if you can, to see if they think these words are pronounced differently or the same. I clearly pronounce the *h*, but my kids don't. And linguists don't know why this is happening. It just is. Gradually, the sound of the *h* in words beginning with *wh* is being dropped. It will make one more spelling conundrum for English-speaking school children who already complain, "Why can't we just spell these words like we *say* them?!"

I Hate to Be Confusing, But...

If only history were neater and less confusing...but, ah, then it wouldn't be nearly as interesting. You remember how King Aethelbert became a Christian when Augustine shared the gospel with him? That's when Christianity came to England...sort of, mostly. You see, there was just a little bit of Christianity already in England that actually got there a wee bit ahead of Augustine. Remember St. Patrick? Ireland became a Christian country because of his missionary work there. Well, eventually Ireland sent out its own missionaries and a man named Columba headed for Scotland to bring those wild Scots and Picts the gospel. Then these new Scottish-style Christians enthusiastically sent missionaries to northern England, Northumbria to be exact. So, now you really had *two* types of Christian missions, monasteries, and churches in England:

1. The Celtic brand coming down from the north to Northumbria

2. The Roman Catholic brand spreading upward from the south

Both of these two different flavors of Christianity grew and spread and were bound for an eventual clash over which would be the rule for England. Was there much of a difference? Basically, it boiled down to some small things like how the monks shaved their heads (I'm not kidding) and the date of Easter on the one hand, and on the other hand, one rather huge thing: church government. It all came to a head at what is known as the Synod of Whitby (a synod is a council meeting) in the year 664. It fell upon the Northumbrian king to break the tie and decide once and for all whether England would go with the Celtic Church and its more loosely organized faith in which power was spread out among all the abbots of the various monasteries, or go with the Roman Catholic Church and its tight organization and strict hierarchy of power with the pope at the top.

The king went with Rome. He figured that would help connect England with the rest of Europe, which was already thoroughly Roman Catholic. Celtic Christianity receded back into Ireland and Scotland. England, from that point on, was Roman Catholic. Many historians feel that in that decision we missed a chance to have an influential, vibrant church in Western Europe that existed separately from the Roman Catholic Church, but which had just as long a tradition. We will never know what that would have been like since it simply didn't happen. Of course, this decision gave the pope in Rome even *more* power. And as the old English saying goes, "Power corrupts, and absolute power corrupts absolutely." How true...as you shall certainly see.

A Monk You Should Know: The Venerable Bede

Around 20 years after the Synod of Whitby, a little boy was born in Northumbria at one of those more Celtic-style monasteries. A birth at a monastery was not too unusual since monasteries were the closest thing to a hospital in those days, and the monks administered medicine and food and other practical helps to the people in the surrounding towns. We don't know anything about the boy's parents, but we do know that when he was just seven years old, he was brought back to the monastery to be raised entirely by the monks. This, too, was not totally uncommon during the Middle Ages. Sometimes parents were too poor to raise a child themselves, or they might simply want to dedicate him to God. This particular boy grew up to become a Benedictine monk and a brilliant scholar. He is known as the Venerable (honorable) Bede, and he certainly deserves to be venerated.

Bede was incredible! All by himself he set the standard—and a very high one—for all historical writing to follow. He was creative, artistic, meticulous, and humble. And best of all, he wrote the very, very first History of England. As you now know, all scholastic writings were in Latin, so his were too. Bede called it the *Ecclesiastica Gentis Anglorum*, Latin for the *Ecclesiastical History of the English People*. "Ecclesiastical" just means having to do with the church, yet his history incorporated so much more than that. Gathering documents and oral testimony from the native English people, he systematically gleaned the best and most reliable and put it all down for us. We would know next to nothing about early England were it not for the Venerable Bede. Also, Bede's history book popularized the system of relating all dates to the birth of Christ by

Small section of a page from an early illuminated copy of Bede's Ecclesiastical History of the English People.

using the term "BC" for *Before Christ*, and "AD" for *Anno Domini*, a Latin phrase for "in the year of our Lord." These Christian designations for historical time periods are quickly giving way today to the more secular terms "BCE," *Before the Common Era*, and "CE," *Common Era*. Nevertheless, the point of transition from one period of time to the other is still right there at the birth of Christ, and Bede helped make it so.

Bede also translated portions of scripture from Latin into English. He was working on the gospel of John when he died. After his death, he was declared a saint by the Catholic Church and, because of the importance of his contribution, he is known today as the Father of English History.

Beowulf

We can't pass through this time period without a look at *Beowulf,* the most widely known classic piece of Old English literature. It's a great tale with dragons, monsters, thanes that get eaten (what's a thane?), and a hero of the highest caliber, Beowulf. All the names have that out-of-the-misty-mountains, hauntingly strange sound to them. *Beowulf* is a massively long poem (3,182 lines) written anywhere from 800 to around 1000 AD. It is an epic story that takes place back in the German hinterlands from whence the Anglo-Saxons came to England. It tells of the warrior Beowulf and his battles against a monster named Grendel and Grendel's mother. Beowulf then becomes a king and eventually ends up fighting a dragon.

In Beowulf you will see *kennings*. A kenning is a compound expression, a compact metaphor, often translated into hyphenated words in modern English. Kennings were used widely in Anglo-Saxon poetry. An example is calling the ocean a *whale-road*. The combination of beauty and imagination embedded in these kennings is one of the chief markings that set Old English poetry apart. Here are just a few of the many imaginative kennings found in Beowulf:

Kenning	Meaning
heath-stalker	deer
ring-giver	king
bone-locks	joints
battle-sweat	blood
soul-slayer	the devil
body-raiment	skin
body-cave	heart
sword-storm	battle

Cædmon's Hymn: A Closer Look at Anglo-Saxon Poetry

A short poem called "Cædmon's Hymn" is another great example of Anglo-Saxon poetry. It was preserved for us by Bede in his history book along with an interesting story about Cædmon, the man who composed it.

According to Bede, Cædmon was a common herdsman who worked at a monastery in Northumbria. All his life he had felt embarrassed about his lack of musical ability. It wouldn't have been so bad except that in his culture at that time it was a custom to pass a harp around the table after supper and take turns entertaining friends and guests with a song. Ashamed of his inability to sing, Cædmon always found an excuse to leave the table before the singing got started. One such night when he had left the table and gone to the stable, he lay down in the hay and fell asleep. He dreamed that someone came to him and said, "Cædmon, sing me something." He responded that he couldn't because he was no good at singing or making up songs. The other person insisted that he sing and told him to sing about creation. Cædmon began to sing and it was a wonderful song. He woke up, wrote down the new song, and from then on Cædmon was always able to write and perform beautiful songs about the Lord. He and the monks at the monastery where he worked believed he had received a gift from God, so Cædmon became a monk in order to devote the rest of his life to writing Christian poetry and songs.

There are other poems and songs that survived from this era that are associated with Cædmon, but there is no proof that he is the author. Only this singular piece can be ascribed to him with assurance. It is the song of creation which he wrote down after his dream. The modern English translation has been inserted underneath each line of Anglo-Saxon. Watch for the kennings Cædmon uses. The spaces in the middle of each line of poetry are explained below. Just read across the space.

Cædmon's Hymn

Nu sculon herigean   heofonrices Weard
Now we must praise   heaven-kingdom's Guardian,

Meotodes meahte   and his modgeþanc
the Creator's might   and his mind-plans,

weorc Wuldor-Fæder   swa he wundra gehwæs
the work of the Glory-Father,   when he of wonders of every one,

ece Drihten   or onstealde
eternal Lord,   the beginning established.

Hærest sceop   ielda bearnum
He first created   for men's sons

heofon to hrofe   halig Scyppend
heaven as a roof,   holy Creator;

ða middangeard   moncynnes Weard
then middle-earth   mankind's Guardian,

ece Drihten   æfter teode
eternal Lord,   afterwards made

firum foldan   Frea aelmihtig
for men earth,   Master almighty.

Besides the kennings, Old English poets loved a poetic device known as alliteration. Alliteration is the repetition of initial word sounds, which you can see throughout this poem. For example, the repeated *m* sound in the second line:

Meotodes meahte   and his modgeþanc

Another definitive aspect of Anglo-Saxon poetry is its meter (the beats). Each line of a poem had a dramatic pause or break in the middle called a *caesura*, and each half-line had to have two, and only two, heavily stressed syllables. Plus, each pair of half-lines had to be connected by alliteration. These poetic rules demanded some fairly tricky word choices. No wonder Cædmon was shy about writing a song.

There are only a few other works in Anglo-Saxon as old as "Caedmon's Hymn," but the authors of these other compositions are unknown (as with *Beowulf*). Cædmon holds the honor of being the earliest known English poet.

�֍✧✧ 𝔄𝔈 ✧✧✧

AD 793.   In this year fierce, foreboding omens came over the land of Northumbria and wretchedly terrified the people. There were excessive whirlwinds, lightning storms, and fiery dragons were seen flying in the sky.

The Anglo-Saxon Chronicle

A Summary of Our History So Far

To Britain

Caesar sailed to Britain small
After he had conquered Gaul.
Thus, Latin mode
Of dress and road
Made its abode
In Britain.

Rome ruled the isle three hundred years
When Constantine Christ's voice did hear.
Soon all Rome claimed
The Savior's name
And spread the flame
To Britain.

'Gainst Rome came Vandals, the German sort,
So Romans left Londinium Fort.
They hearkened home
To fight for Rome,
Abandoned stone
Of Britain.

'Cross whale-road Anglo-Saxons came
To loot and burn then plant their name.
Their tongue, you see,
Old English be.
Must die or flee
Now, Britons!

Bold Britons shot and stabbed and bled,
Fought all they could and then they fled,
And Christian Celts
Like Arthur knelt
To what God dealt
To Britain.

Thanking Thor, the conquering men
Beckoned their Germanic kin:
"Come, take some land,
Lend a hand,
Make Angle-land
Of Britain!"

Alas, sweet isle's de-gospelled sod
Lay once again in need of God.
Though dark the scene,
Light intervened...
Sailed Augustine
To Britain.

The Invasion of the Vikings and Old Norse

Chapter 5

Wake early
if you want
another man's life or land.
No lamb
for the lazy wolf.
No battle's won in bed.

From *The Havamal*,
A medieval manuscript in Old Norse

The Original Meaning of Berserk

The Anglo-Saxons began invading England in the 400's, and they had to work awhile to push out those Celts. Finally, they were all happily nestled into their shires (Anglo-Saxon for *counties*) when another group of foreigners began invading. The invaders got invaded, so to speak. The new invaders were infamous pirates known as the Norsemen, or the Danes. But do these names ring a bell? Perhaps not. These are names historians use, and you should know them. But the men who led the raiding parties of these particular folk, the pirates who came just to get the loot and leave before any of their people even thought of coming to settle down and stay, these men (and a few women) were known first and foremost as the Vikings.

The term Viking usually conjures up certain images: large ships with fearsome dragonheads on the prow; blond, heavy-set, wild warriors wielding huge axes; tough, cold-hardened men who plunder helpless villages and are proud of it. Well, if that's your image, you nailed them. Their war ships were called longships because they were exceedingly long compared to everyone else's and intimidating looking on the horizon. These ships also had rudders, giving them superior maneuverability compared to other European ships of the day. Vikings were, indeed, generally blond or red-haired with blue eyes and fair skin. They came from some of the coldest regions of the world and looked like nothing could make them shiver. They plundered, burned, looted, raped, murdered, enslaved and terrorized across the globe—France, England, Scotland, Ireland, Germania, Russia, even Siberia—anywhere there were coastal areas that could be reached by their longships. Basically, if your country had beachfront property, you were vulnerable to attack by Vikings.

The term *Norsemen* comes from *north-men* since these people were from the northernmost parts of Europe: Iceland, Norway, Sweden, and Denmark. Those from Denmark were also referred to as the *Danes*. The language of Norse, or Old Norse as we call it today, was the language of all these Norse-folk, though there were many regional variations and dialects. However, just because these people held the same basic religion, language, and way of life, don't think they weren't fighting each other. Much of the history of these countries involves battles among themselves and a constant striving for supremacy and rule among all the Viking tribes and kingdoms.

They were known for being wild in battle, and there were some among them, both men and women, called *berserkers*, who went absolutely insane in battle. They went into a feverish frenzy, whacking and kicking, stabbing and grinding their teeth. That's where our word *berserk* comes from. Some historians think these berserkers were eating a certain type of plant that contained a hallucinogenic drug that would make a person go into this type of frenzy, but that has not been proven. Language-wise, the word *berserk* is just the beginning of the Old Norse influence upon English. The Vikings' language would invade our own in many ways over the next few centuries.

King Alfred

These medieval pirates had an extensive and lucrative slave trade going on, and as they pillaged and burned and captured slaves to sell all over the world, they decided to also start some permanent settlements. It was mainly the Danish Vikings of Denmark, whose land was a short trip across the sea from England, who began to look longingly at the English countryside as an ideal place for their own farms and families. So they began trying to do to the Anglo-Saxons just what the Anglo-Saxons had done to the Celts—one of those classic instances where history repeats itself. They were burning and looting the monasteries as they began taking land, slaughtering people or taking them as slaves, wreaking ghastly havoc upon the unfortunates who got in their way. The Anglo-Saxons were having a very hard time holding their own. The Danes began to capture whole swaths of territory beginning in the north with Northumbria. Then, by around 850 AD, large armies of Danish Viking parties with fleets of ships were coming as far south as London and Canterbury. Then, they started to move west. It was beginning to look like the Anglo-Saxons might, indeed, lose the land they had won just a few centuries before. But we know that didn't happen. After all, we speak English and not Danish in America today.

Alas, as in all good fairy tales, and sometimes on very special occasions in real life, the right man comes along at just the right time and saves the day. Thus it happened for England at this time, and the man was Alfred. Alfred was the youngest son born to the King of Wessex, or West Saxons. He had three older brothers who were in line to inherit the throne, so he never expected to be king. His early years were focused on scholarly pursuits, and as it turned out, Alfred excelled as a student. But Alfred was a warrior, too, as were his brothers, and they were all engaged in the fight to stop the Danish invasion.

As the Vikings encroached farther into England, Alfred watched as two of his older brothers died in succession after taking the throne. Now, with his remaining brother Aethelred as king, Alfred began leading battle after battle in the continued effort to check the enemy's advance. Then, to the dismay of all, King Aethelred was killed at the Battle of Merton. It was one of the lowest points in history for the Anglo-Saxons. The Danes now controlled all the English territories but Wessex. At this pivotal time in the history of England, twenty-three-year-old Alfred was thrust into being king of Wessex after all. He took the throne in 871 AD and began to mount a strong, carefully planned campaign against the Danes. Finally, after seven more years of struggle, he accomplished what his father and his brothers had not been able to do. Through a series of victories, he forced the Danes to surrender, and terms for peace were reached at last.

The treaty allowed the Vikings to stay in the northern part of England but required them to get out of Wessex. Also, part of the agreement was that they would become Christians. The Danish king was baptized along with many of his men. The area given to the Vikings consisted of parts of Northumbria, Mercia, and East Anglia (see map on p. 28). Because this territory was now officially under the rule or law of the Vikings, and because these particular Vikings happened to be the Danes, their land became known as Danelaw. So the Vikings, or Danes, were there to stay, but at least they had agreed to keep their settlements within the boundaries of Danelaw.

Statue of Alfred the Great at Winchester, England, ancient capital of Wessex

By this time, it was obvious that Alfred had wonderful qualities of leadership, courage, and vision, and there was a general desire among the English to unite under his rule. Thus, he became the very first king of all England. He also became known as Alfred the Great, the only English king to be designated as such. And what a truly great king he was! First he rebuilt and restored those English towns and monasteries that had suffered rampant destruction in the wars with the Danes. He reorganized the government to make it more efficient and wrote a lasting legal code called the *Book of Dooms*. According to Winston Churchill in his *Birth of Britain*, Alfred's law code blended the best ideas from Christian, Old Germanic, and Mosaic (Moses') law.

Trained as a scholar, Alfred encouraged learning, promoted schools, and most important of all for our study, he promoted English. He wanted the various English tribes to feel unified, and what better way to do that, he thought, than to publish a history of England *in English* not Latin. He knew that encouraging pride in their common language and in the history of their island home would certainly promote a feeling of national pride and oneness among the people. Alfred himself translated Bede's *Ecclesiastical History of the English People* from Bede's scholarly Latin text into common, scruffy, everyday English. Then he commissioned the writing of the very first complete history of England in English, and it was called the *Anglo-Saxon Chronicle*. The *Chronicle* began with Rome's invasion of Britain, leaning heavily on Bede's work for the very early history and continuing on up to Alfred's day. From that point onward, the *Chronicle* became an ongoing record of important events and people, and it was kept current for centuries beyond Alfred's life and rule. The *Anglo-Saxon Chronicle* remains our richest source for everything about the early Middle Ages in England.

As part of his plan to promote learning, Alfred became the first ruler in all of history to make the ability to read and write one of the qualifications for a nobleman. He established a system of courts based on shires (counties), and kept administrative policies so well defined and workable that some historians claim that England had the most advanced government in Western Europe at this time.

Known for his humility, faith, and his desire to serve the English people, King Alfred was, indeed, the right man who came along at just the right time. He had preserved Christian England from complete subjugation to the pagan Vikings and, quoting Churchill again: "[Alfred] had by policy and arms preserved the Christian civilization in England."

This silver coin was struck around 880 AD during Alfred's reign to honor him. It reads Ælfred Rex, but the words are divided in an odd way with "Ælfr" on the left and "ed Rex" on the right. Also, the X is much smaller than the other letters. The Æ is a symbol no longer used in modern English that carried the short sound of "a." Rex is Latin for king.

King Cnut

From here on there's good news and bad news. The bad news is, even though the English held the Danes in check for a while, the Danes made a comeback, a big one. Several Danish kings in a row began capturing and conquering again until England was forced to pay Danegeld, or taxes, to the Danish government. Eventually, the whole affair culminated in a Danish king for England about a hundred years after Alfred's reign. He was a Christian king named Cnut (pronounced ka-**noot**), and he held not only Denmark and England, but also Norway and part of Sweden, too, putting them under one rule. Thus, the island was subjected to foreign rule for the first time since the Romans ruled the Britons.

But there was good news, too. The good news was that the English people were established in England forever now, and it was just a question of to whom they owed their allegiance, and to whom they paid their taxes. There was no question now of being driven out. Also, the Danes had made great strides in their own culture and government during the past century, and Cnut turned out to be a wonderful king. Danish rule was enlightened and well managed. As the Danish government combined with the English law established by Alfred, England prospered. Besides, the Danes were not in control for long.

Old Norse Meets Old English

From the time of Danelaw, a lot of intermingling began to take place between the Danes and the English. English merchants and sea captains transacted business with the Danes. English farmers sold their vegetables to neighboring Danish farmers. Danish and English young people began to marry each other. Thus, the Old Norse language invaded the Old English through all this intermingling of life and love.

First, Old English adopted lots of Old Norse words. If a word begins with or contains an *sk* or *sc* (when *sc* is pronounced like *sk*) there's a good chance it is an adoption from the Old Norse. Words such as—

scarf	skate
scare	skid
scale	skill
scrape	skip
score	skirt
scrub	sky

Sometimes English adopted the Old Norse and still kept the Old English for the same word. Then we ended up with two words pretty much for the same thing: *shirt* and *skirt*, for example. At one time these words both referred to the same clothing piece. Can you tell which one is Old Norse? *Skirt*— it begins with *sk*. Another example is *hide* and *skin*. Which is Old Norse? You bet—*skin*.

Here are some more doubles for the same thing:

Anglo-Saxon	Old Norse
no	nay
rear	raise
from	fro (as in "swing to and *fro*")
craft	skill
sick	ill
shatter	scatter
shriek	screech
ditch	dyke

You have to be careful not to think that just any word with an "sk" is Old Norse. But it is a good guess. If you want to be sure, though, you have to look it up. There are also words like *skew* and *skim* that come to us from Old French.

I counted 33 root *sk* words in my dictionary. By "root" I mean that I counted *sky* only once, and not the words *skyline, skylark, skylight*, etc., and I counted *skimp*, but not *skimpy*. Of those 33 root words, 16 were Old Norse in origin. That's close enough to call it half. French was next with 9, and the rest were divided among Greek, Native American (skunk), and various colloquial or slang expressions that don't have long histories.

Over a thousand place names came into the English from Old Norse, too. All place names that end in *–by*, such as *Appleby* (also as in the chain restaurant *Applebees*), *Darby*, and *Grimesby* are Old Norse. We know this because the ending *-by* meant town or farm in Old Norse. Also, *thorpe* meant village, so we have place names ending with *–thorpe*, too. Thus, when you read that a General *Oglethorpe* from England founded the colony of Georgia in the 1700's, you know that his ancestors most likely came from a town that was named by some old Norseman. Because America was settled by the English, all these various Norse names survive here, too. So, we have both place names and family names here in America that come straight from the Vikings. Perhaps, your family, town, or street is among them.

Lots of common words dropped in from the Danes, words such as:

awkward	bank	cast	birth
freckle	dirt	egg	guess
gasp	get	nag	kindle
knife	rugged	scowl	weak

Not only were words picked up, but also the grammar was affected. This was not really true with the influence from Latin. Latin greatly expanded the vocabulary of English, but that is all. Old Norse had a much deeper influence in that it helped simplify the syntax (sentence formation) and morphology (word formation) of our language. Also, in many instances, the Norse word completely replaced the Anglo-Saxon word, which also reflects an influence at a deeper level.

As we mentioned earlier, Anglo-Saxon was originally a highly inflected language. This means that inflections in words determined the meaning of a sentence. For instance, look at these words:

likes, Sarah, me

If I told you to arrange them and make a sentence of those words, you'd say, "Sarah likes me," and not "Me likes Sarah." That's because pronouns are still inflected in English and *me* is an inflection of the pronoun *I*. When you hear *me* instead of *I*, you assume that *me* is the object not the subject of the sentence; that is, it receives the "liking." You also assume that Sarah is the subject and is doing the "liking." Now, consider:

like, Sarah, I

The meaning is immediately changed with just the switch of *me* to *I*. Now, you would (I hope) write the sentence as "I like Sarah." Did you catch the other change? *Likes* has become *like*, and that is another inflection. That little shift of adding the -*s* is one more clue to the meaning. Well, think of a language in which every single word changed its form or ending when it shifted its purpose in a sentence. *That's* an inflected language.

English is no longer considered an inflected language. We still use some inflections, as with the pronouns above, but today English is considered to be an analytical language, which means word order is more important than inflections. Word order determines meaning. So, when I say,

"My sister hit my friend," you know who was hitting whom by the word order and not because I put some kind of case ending on *sister* or *friend*.

This is a long way of saying that as Old Norse intermingled with Old English, the two simplified each other. Old Norse helped English along the path toward fewer inflections. Both languages were from the Germanic branch of Indo-European languages, so if an Englishman and a Norseman worked at it, they could almost understand each other. Many words were similar enough to help them get their point across. You know the way we simplify our speech when talking to a foreigner who doesn't speak good English? We might say: "I go to store. You go, too?" Well, picture an English farmer talking Old English to his Old-Norse-speaking neighbor and trying to make himself understood. You get the idea. It's sort of the Anglo-Saxon version of, "Me Tarzan, you Jane."

Then, don't forget to factor in the basic rule of all language change:

Living languages always simplify over time.

English was destined to simplify anyway. Close contact with the Old Norse just hurried it up a bit.

✠✠✠ Æ ✠✠✠

AD 900. Alfred, son of Aethelwulf, passed away six nights before All Saints Day. He was king over all the English, except for that part which was under Danish rule; and he held that kingdom for one and a half years less than thirty.

The Anglo-Saxon Chronicle

Part III

Middle English

1066—1500

The Battle of Hastings, which occurred in 1066, formed the dividing mark between the early and the late Middle Ages. This battle also ushered in the greatest influence yet upon our tongue...
ever heard of *Frenglish*?

The Invasion of the Normans

and Old French

Chapter 6

AD 1066. Then came William, eorl of Normandy, into Pevensey on Michaelmas eve, and as soon as they were prepared, they built a stronghold at the town of Hastings.

The Anglo-Saxon Chronicle

William the Conqueror

At this point we have to back up just a bit and let me fill you in on some tidbits of history concerning France. France was called Gaul under Roman rule. The name France is from the Germanic tribe of Franks that invaded there, just as England got its name from its German invaders. The Latin language had taken root in Gaul among all the people, and then as the Franks settled in, the Latin spoken there became influenced by the Franks resulting in the Romance language of French, Old French to be exact. So, while the English were speaking Old English, the French were speaking Old French.

French was and still is a beautiful language. It has always been generally regarded as one of the most beautiful languages of the world. Thus, when a group of Danish Vikings started plundering and then settling on the northern shores of France, they fell in love with the French language. In fact, they loved it so much, they gave up speaking their own

language of Old Norse. In just one generation they had completely abandoned Old Norse, and if their children learned it at all, it was as a second
language. Historians say this is unheard of, a kind of world record for
defaulting on your native tongue. These Viking settlers loved everything
about the French culture and rapidly assimilated every aspect they could
into their own ways. Since they were Norse-men, or North-men, this got
slurred into Nor-men...Norman. They became known as the Norman
French and their land was called Normandy.

"Normandy," you may say to yourself, "I've heard of that." Indeed,
you probably have. It is the strip of land in France where the Allied forces
landed on D-Day in World War II. On that day—July 6, 1944—American,
British, and Canadian troops crossed the English Channel and landed in
Normandy for the largest military invasion by sea in all of history. When
anyone says, "Normandy" today, D-Day is the first thing that comes to
most people's mind.

The French king liked the Normans and appointed their king to be
the Duke of Normandy, a huge mark of respect. The Duke of Normandy
retained his rule over Normandy, but he paid allegiance to the King of
France. Meanwhile, he also kept up relations with his Viking kinfolk,
specifically the Danes, who were ruling over England at this time. One of
these Danish-English kings married a princess from Normandy. There was
a lot of intermarrying of royal lines going on.

From there on, I'll spare you the details. Suffice it to say that eventually the Anglo-Saxons got to rule over themselves in England again, but
only for about twenty years. The king of that brief time was Anglo-Saxon,
but he had connections (including loose kinship ties) to the Norman
French. When he died leaving no direct heirs to the throne of England,
William, the Duke of Normandy (one of those who were loosely kin)
claimed that the throne of England should rightfully be his.

The English resisted. They wanted one of their own to be king, a
nobleman named Harold, the Earl of Wessex. They sure didn't want to go
from years of Danish rule to French rule!

Nevertheless, on October 14 in the year 1066 at the Battle of Hastings, the French-speaking Duke of Normandy overwhelmed Harold and his
Anglo-Saxon forces. Harold was killed, William won the English crown
that day, and, along with the title of king of England, he became known as
William the Conqueror who conquered England.

From this point on, England's ties with the Vikings, Denmark, and Old Norse began to fade. A new invasion of the English language had begun and the effect would be enormous, and the impact would be from French.

This picture is a small section of a tapestry, the Bayeux Tapestry of Normandy, France, commissioned by William the Conqueror around 1070. It depicts Harold's death at the Battle of Hastings. You can see the name of Harold in the upper right corner.

Language du Jour

After the Battle of Hastings, William brought a whole entourage of French speaking aristocrats into England to be his royal court and to fill any and all of the important positions of the government and the church. In other words, anyone who was anybody was French. A few of these Norman French learned English as a second language, but not many—there was no real need. French alone was spoken in all the schools and in the homes of the upper class, in all government proceedings and court-room business. The only exception was the use of Latin in the religious sector. The English language was considered crass and vulgar. The word *vulgar* here means common, not nasty. However, the French almost put English in the nasty category.

Just as most of us would be, the defeated English people were eager to impress those above them on the social ladder, and the top rungs of this ladder were now solidly French. People began throwing in French phrases and words, mixing them with regular English. Everyone wanted to sound and look as French as possible. One historian jokingly suggested that we call the English spoken during this period "Frenglish" because it was such a complete mixture of French and English.

Believe it or not, all this foolishness got carried on for a very long time, centuries in fact. One can see the remnants of these things even today. A small, down-home restaurant might offer the *soup of the day;* whereas a restaurant aiming at more sophisticated customers would call it *soupe du jour.* That little bit of un-translated French adds cultural spice to the menu. The same thing applies to *à la carte* and *à la mode.* If you think about it, the whole industry of fashion is saturated with words *en Français,* from *coiffure* for hairstyle, to *lingerie* for undergarments. French design equals style, and as most people know, Paris has been seen as the cultural center for trend-setting for decades. But what people don't know is that it's really been centuries. In fact, the cultural compass that points to France for sophistication was calibrated at the Battle of Hastings back in 1066 AD!

So, over nine hundred years ago the ladies in England were worrying about what the ladies in Paris were wearing. But the French people who lived in and around Paris made fun of the Norman French who lived in England. They thought of the Normans as French wanna-be's. They even made fun of their Norman accent. To guard against being seen as gauche (that's French for tacky), Norman-French-speaking folk who lived in England often sent their children off to schools in Paris so the kids would speak a better brand of French. People really haven't changed a bit, have they?

The Abandoned Chronicle

Poor King Alfred! He had made English such a respectable language in his day. He had worked hard to unite all English speaking people and to give them pride in their native tongue. He had been the catalyst for the Anglo-Saxon Chronicle being written in English not Latin, a very big deal back then. Now, all that effort seemed wasted. In fact, about a hundred years after William did his conquering, the monks gave up keeping the Anglo-Saxon Chronicle altogether. No histories were being written in English anymore. No scholarly things at all were being written in English. If they were not in French, they were back to being in Latin again. Because French was a Romance language and, thus, a descendant of Latin anyway, the French had continued to keep their scholarly works in Latin. This put Latin back in its position of supremacy, with French as its handmaiden. So, into English came this huge new influx of Latin words along with all this suffocatingly rich, high-calorie French. But English was lean and hearty. And, as it turned out, it did not suffocate. It grew.

✠✠✠ Æ ✠✠✠

AD 1087.   Alas, how false and how unsteady is this middle-earth's pros-
perity. He who was before a powerful king and lord of many
lands, had of all land only the measure of seven feet; and
he who was at times clothed with gold and gems, he lay then
covered over with earth.

Comment on the death and burial of William the Conqueror
The Anglo-Saxon Chronicle

The Making of Middle English

Chapter 7

Full wise is he that can himselven knowe.

From "The Monk's Tale,"
The Canterbury Tales, Geoffrey Chaucer

The Beginning of the Middle

With the general take-over by the Norman French, the English language began to change so greatly that linguists put the English spoken during this period into a completely separate category. Of course, on the day of the Battle of Hastings, the Anglo-Saxons didn't suddenly start pronouncing their words differently, nor did they gain hundreds of new French words at the moment of surrender. However, the change by linguistic standards happened so quickly and was so huge that from the time of the Battle of Hastings to the time of the Renaissance around 1500, the English spoken is no longer designated as Old English. It is Middle English from this point onward until the close of the Middle Ages. Naturally, the people from that period didn't call it anything but English. They didn't know they were the middle period of anything. As far as they knew, they were speaking the latest lingo and the most modern English ever.

Losing Our Gutturals

There are around eighty sounds we humans make and use for our various languages. Interestingly, English uses only forty of these. What sounds are we missing? Well, clicks, for instance. The Hottentots, a tribe in Africa, put clicking sounds in their speech. Linguists have had a hard time figuring out how they even produce these sounds while they talk, and just think of trying to devise a way to write it down. One of the greatest challenges for Bible translators, in fact, has been finding new symbols to represent the sounds in some of these highly unusual languages. (If you want to hear some of this click-talk, check out the classic independent film *The Gods Must Be Crazy*. The story involves a tribe of Hottentots who talk with these clicks, and they hired real natives to play the parts.)

Another sound we do not make is one that we actually once made in English. However, it was during the Middle English period that it disappeared as people began to drop it out of their speech. Ever wonder why in the world we have a word that we pronounce *nite* but spell *night*? Well, that silent *gh* was once pronounced. In fact, almost all the unpronounced letters in English were at one time pronounced. English used to be spelled pretty much the way it was spoken.

That *gh* sound was one of the hand-me-down sounds from English's Germanic days. Remember, English is in the Germanic branch of the Indo-European Family of Languages. All Germanic languages have that sound. It's known as a guttural, meaning the sound is a throaty one, like our *h* mixed with a little bit of *k*, and sounding a bit like someone clearing his throat. The word *night* was pronounced with the *n* as in modern English, but then a short *i* (as in *hit*), and a slight guttural sound for the *gh* and then the *t*. *Night* rhymed with *fit* or *hit*, and so did the word *knight* in which the *k* also was pronounced. Try saying *knight* with all these changes in pronunciation and see what it sounds like... "*K-ni-gh(guttural)-t.*"

Why did this *gh* sound get dropped? It was because there were no guttural sounds in French. The French had trouble pronouncing it when (if at all) they attempted to speak English. And the English wanted so badly to imitate this seemingly more cultured language of the new ruling class, they could not escape the urge to soften and eventually drop the rude, crude Germanic sounds from their common speech. From the time of the Battle of Hastings to the end of the Middle English Period, those sounds gradually disappeared.

WH and CW Bite the Dust

It was mentioned earlier that the original *hw* of Old English got switched around to our modern *wh*. This shift happened during the Middle English period. Similarly, another switch-a-roo occurred as *cw* was exchanged for *qu*. The French had no *cw* in their language and so the Old English spelling was soon shifted to the fashionably French *qu*. Hw is more accurate to our actual pronunciation of that sound, and *cw* seems plainer and simpler, but who cares for accurate and simple when sophistication and fashion are at stake? Hwerever they went and hwatever they did, the upper and middle class English were cwite determined to learn to dress and talk and act as French as they could as cwickly as possible. And they did. And you spell and pronounce your words differently today because of it.

From Hog in the Barnyard to Pork on the Table

A gentleman landowner might speak English to the peasant who worked on the noble's farm, or to the maid in the kitchen, but the minute he began dealing with other landowners, or merchants, or clergy, or government officials, he spoke French. So the animal we know as a hog was, indeed, a hog while he was in the barnyard, while he was cared for by an English-speaking commoner who called it a hog. Then the hog got butchered and cooked, and served at the master's table. Now, voila! It was no longer a hog. It was pork. Hog is the Anglo-Saxon word and pork is the French. So, if you ever thought it was odd that we call some meats by one name as the animal and something different when it reaches the table, now you know—it all goes back to William the Conqueror in 1066. Here are a few more:

Anglo-Saxon	French
cow........	beef
deer.......	venison
sheep.....	mutton
calf........	veal

And chicken? Somehow the chicken escaped. We call it chicken in the barnyard as well as on the table. However, we do often use the French word for it too—*poultry*.

French greatly expanded our vocabulary in other areas besides food giving us other word doubles to use for the same thing. For instance:

Anglo-Saxon	French
wish..........	desire
stench.......	odor
might........	power

ask............	request
shun.........	avoid
look.........	spy
stream......	river
limb.........	branch
song.........	ballad

With English now having borrowed from three different language sources (Latin, Old Norse, and French), we even ended up with words in triplicate for the same thing. For instance, we've already looked at *hide* and *skin*, with *hide* being Anglo-Saxon and *skin* Old Norse. Now, the French added the word *pelt* giving us three words that all mean basically the same thing. *Sack* (Latin), *bag* (Old Norse), and *pouch* (Old French) are another example.

Unlike Norse, the influence of French is not considered an in-depth influence; that is, it did not change the grammar of our language as much as Old Norse. Nevertheless, it virtually doubled our vocabulary. English has added so many French words that estimates range from 30-50% on the proportion of English words derived from French. So, I won't try to enumerate much more on which words. Suffice it to say that you can pick up any dictionary and see for yourself that almost every other root word is derived from French.

One more thing that should be re-emphasized here is that French itself is derived from Latin. It is a Romance language. Thus many words in English that have a Latin root came in through the Old French. Some Latin words hopped straight from Latin into English by way of the church or science or some other intellectual pursuit. But others came roundabout via Old French. When you spot one of these words in a dictionary that shows word origins (as many do), it will show you something like this: [O.Fr.< Latin] meaning the word is from the Old French and the Old French got it from the Latin. Comprenez-vous?

The Hundred Years' War

The English found themselves taking the French nobles' word for it that their own English tongue was neither as beautiful nor as flexible as French. They were even convinced that English was too crude and lowly to express the finer points of philosophy, law, or religion. Truly. They actually thought this! English was considered an inferior language in every respect.

What the English language needed was another revival, a revival like the one under King Alfred. Alfred had understood that to encourage a national feeling of patriotism, a people needed to feel proud of their native language. But was there anything strong enough to dam up this linguistic tidal wave of French? A war, perhaps? Well, that's just what happened.

When William the Conqueror became king of England, he was also the Duke of Normandy, and the Duke of Normandy was a vassal to the King of France. Being a vassal state of France meant you had to pay the French king some taxes. So picture William, king of England now, still ruling in Normandy, too, and having to pay taxes for Normandy to the King of France. Anyone might guess that this was a set-up for an inevitable big political fuss. As William's descendants took the throne after him over the next few centuries, no one was satisfied with things as they were. Both France and England wanted to extend their lands on the Normandy side of the English Channel. Tensions mounted as England and France entered a long-term power struggle over who would control these lands, lands that were all part of what we call France today (a clue as to who finally won). These disputed territories included Normandy itself, along with some others, such as the duchies of Anjou and Aquitaine. A duchy is a state ruled by a duke who owes allegiance to a king somewhere, in this case either France or England. Ownership of these duchies kept shifting back and forth as France and England vied for power and control. At one point, in fact, the king of England actually held more territory "in France" than did the King of France!

Finally, under the reign of Edward III of England, the disputes erupted into full-scale war. From 1337 until 1453, a little over a century, England and France engaged in what is known as the Hundred Years' War. This long, ongoing war with France gradually fostered a rising English patriotism. Over the years, the nobility had begun to intermarry with the English quite a bit, and most of them now spoke English on the side. Finally, it occurred to them that there could be no better way to demonstrate one's patriotism than to give up speaking the language of the enemy and begin speaking the language of one's homeland. So, that's what they did. The government began to encourage English. School children were instructed to do their lessons in English. English supplanted French in the king's court, in the law courts, and in all government business. In fact, speaking English became like waving the English flag, and the English people could do it every time they opened their mouth.

Spurned by aristocrats and relegated to the peasant class for almost four hundred years, the English language was humble and lowly, yet alive and supple, too. It had been nurtured in the fertile field of the everyday talk of common folk. Its roots ran deep in the soil of its island home. Now, at last, as it grew back up to prominence, it was like a spreading tree, dense in the heartwood of its German stock and rich in recent new growth from the influence of French. With the Renaissance on the horizon, the sap of new ideas was already running up to all its branches and was getting them ready to bear the fruit of some of the greatest literature the world has ever known.

Geoffrey Chaucer

Geoffrey Chaucer is the best known author of the Middle English period. He is considered to be England's first great poet. It is appropriate, considering the time in which he lived, that his name is French, from the word *chaussier*, meaning *shoemaker*, probably an occupation of one of his ancestors. Chaucer grew up in a prosperous family who were part of an up and coming new class of people—the middle class. He was born close to the time that the Hundred Years' War began. Up until his generation, school students were asked to translate their Latin assignments into French. Chaucer was probably among the first students who were instructed to translate their Latin into English, a change brought on by the new feeling of patriotism due to the war. In 1362, by the time Chaucer was around 20 years old, Parliament ordered that English was to be used in all judicial proceedings and trials. The nobility continued to speak French among themselves, but the days of French were numbered and Chaucer helped to escort it out.

Chaucer, like most of the middle and upper class people of his day, was fluent in Latin and French as well, but he chose to compose all his works in English. By doing so, he brought awareness to commoner and noble alike that the English language was packed with potential for great writing.

The Canterbury Tales, Chaucer's most famous work, was a huge success. In it, Chaucer tells the story of a group of people on a pilgrimage to a religious shrine in Canterbury, England. In order to pass the time, they agree to take turns telling stories to the group. This setting allowed Chaucer to include many varied stories told by a wide range of characters from all walks of life. Though unintentional at the time, Chaucer couldn't have picked a better set-up for introducing later generations to

The pilgrims gather around a table for supper at an inn in this 1483 woodcut from Chaucer's *Canterbury Tales*. Printed in London by William Caxton.

the life and times of the 1300's. Along with the value of his work to historians, Chaucer's crisp and original rhymes, his humor and insights into human nature, his clever pokes at every level of society, all went into making *The Canterbury Tales* some of the best narrative poems ever written in English. Because of his deep influence and popularity, Chaucer is known as the father of English Literature.

John Wycliffe and the First English Bible

By the close of the Middle Ages seeds had been sown for a religious movement which was to bring about a deep transition in politics, society, and most of all, the church. John Wycliffe (**wĭck**-liff) was an early reformer who helped sow those seeds.

Wycliffe lived at just about the same time as Chaucer (late 1300's). He went to Oxford University in England as a theology student and then became a teacher there. As a theology student, he was able for the first time to read the scriptures for himself. The Bible was in its Latin prison, as you may recall, and because Bibles were handwritten, they were rare. Very few men had both access to the scriptures and the education to read them.

Wycliffe began to discover truths in the Bible that he thought the Roman Catholic Church had twisted. He became convinced that if everyone could just read the Bible for themselves they would see the same errors he saw in the Church's teachings. He began to talk openly, expressing his views to the other faculty members. He wrote articles arguing for translations into the common languages of Europe, especially English. The Church taught that the Bible should only be read by scholars and priests and then carefully interpreted to the common man. It was commonly believed that if every man (and worse yet, every woman) could read it for himself, people might get all sorts of wrong or dangerous ideas. Wycliffe seemed to be living proof of their fears as he attacked the Catholic view of the pope and other teachings of the Church that he believed were in serious error.

Wycliffe was brilliant and very persuasive. At first, as people listened to him and agreed, the university itself proudly stood by him. Then the pope got wind of what Wycliffe was teaching and preaching. He demanded that Wycliffe be arrested. The faculty at Oxford did not go along with the pope and refused to have him arrested, but Wycliffe was dismissed as a professor. He had gathered a devout following of men and women by that time (they were called the Lollards), and several of them with Wycliffe's help and guidance, began working on an English translation of the Bible. All the work was done by hand.

John Wycliffe at work in his study.

But slowly, page-by-page, copies were made and distributed along with tracts and pamphlets explaining the Lollards' views that the church needed reforming. For the rest of his life, Wycliffe's focus was getting the Bible into the language of the common man and woman.

The handwritten Bible that Wycliffe and his followers labored to copy was the very first complete Bible in the English language. It was a translation from Latin. Although the New Testament was originally written in Greek and the Old Testament in Hebrew, Wycliffe did not have Greek or Hebrew manuscripts available to him as biblical translators do today. The Latin Vulgate Bible was the only one available in Western Europe at this time. So Wycliffe's English Bible was a translation of a translation, but it was in English and that's all that mattered. The common English man or woman could read it.

After Wycliffe's death, an English council of the church decided he had been a heretic after all. His writings were officially condemned as heresy; his Bibles, along with his many essays, were gathered and burned. From then on anyone caught possessing Wycliffe's Bibles or books could be charged with heresy and executed. And, as if all that wasn't enough, the church council ordered his bones dug up, crushed, and dumped into a river. But they could not dig his influence out of the hearts and minds of those who had heard him preach or had read his opinions. It was just a matter of time before these very ideas would come to fruition, and next time there would be no way to stop them.

John Wycliffe is often called the Morning Star of the Reformation, and the Reformation was, indeed, about to break forth with its great light of truth and freedom upon the continent of Europe and the island kingdom of England. But truth is dangerous, and freedom almost always comes with a price. The use of English instead of French was definitely on the upswing in England, but it was going to be a tough battle to get the truths of scripture into English. The hierarchy of the Catholic Church was not going to give up without a fight.

From Fæder to Fadir

Let's look at the Lord's Prayer again. We will compare the Old English with the Middle English. The Middle English version is from Wycliffe's English Bible. It is dated around 1384, which is also right at the time of Chaucer.

As you read it, notice how the letter thorn (þ) is still in use in the Middle English version for the *th* sound. But, the Old English eth (ð), which was also for *th*, is no longer there, and the ash [æ] is gone as well, though the ash still showed up off and on for centuries. The words are a little more readable to our modern eyes. Most of all, notice how the Old English beginning, *Father our*, has been switched to the modern word order of *Our Father*. English is making its transition from an inflected language to an analytical language in which word order, not inflections, determine meaning. The English language changed more during the Middle English period than at any other time.

Old English	Middle English
Fæder ure þu þe eart on heofonum	Oure fadir þat art in heuenes
si þin nama gehalgod;	halwid be þi name;
tobecume þin rice,	þi kyngdom come to be,
gewurþe ðin willa	Be þi wille don
on eorðan swa swa on heofonum.	in herþe as it is dounin heuene.
urne gedæghwamlican hlaf syle us todæg,	yeue to us today oure eche dayes bred,
and forgyf us ure gyltas	And foryeue to us oure dettis þat is oure synnys
swa swa we forgyfað urum gyltendum	as we foryeuen to oure dettouris þat is to men þat han synned in us;
and ne gelæd þu us on costnunge ac alys us of yfele soþlice.	And lede us not into temptacion but delyuere us from euyl.

Some Þoughts On Þ

It seems a shame that we lost our letter þorn. Just þink how we could have had þis one single letter in many of our words raþer than having to deal wiþ boþ *t* and *h* all þe time. Þere are literally þousands of words þat þis would have shortened! What would it be like if we could use þorn wiþ modern English? We could easily fit a þorn key onto our computer keyboards. And just þink how useful it would be wiþ texting and IM's—can you faþom þat? I really þink þey þrew out a good þing.

✠✠✠ Æ ✠✠✠

John Wycliffe translated the gospel...from Latin into the English. What was previously known only by learned clerics and those of good understanding has become common, and available to the laity, in fact, even to women who can read. As a result, the pearls of the gospel have been scattered and spread before swine.

Henry Knighton, English chronicler, protesting Wycliffe's Bible
Quoted by Alister McGrath in his book *In The Beginning*

And the Word Became...Print!

Chapter 8

What gunpowder did for war
the printing press has done for the mind.

Wendell Phillips

Johannes Gutenberg

John Wycliffe and his followers labored long hours copying the Bible into English by hand. What Wycliffe had needed so badly was a way to mass-produce his English Bibles. But Wycliffe died while book production methods remained the same.

Then in 1456 a German by the name of Johannes Gutenberg invented a thing called movable type and the first printing press was born. Just as the invention of the computer has changed our communications forever, so the invention of the printing press totally transformed communications for the world of that era. Handwritten books were rare and expensive, but printed books were affordable even to the middle class. So almost overnight books began to appear everywhere and everyone wanted books, books, and more books.

Besides hand copying, the only other process for producing a book at that time was by using large wooden blocks. Each block would have all the letters of a page individually carved into it, and then the block was used like a giant stamp as it was swabbed in ink and pressed onto a page. Wooden blocks were time consuming to carve (to say the least) and, once carved, could only be used to reproduce that individual page of the book. A new block had to be hand-carved for each page. This process was an improvement on hand copying in some ways, but books produced by woodblocks were still tedious to produce and, therefore, still so expensive that very few could afford them.

With the advent of the printing press, the process of getting letters on a page was radically changed by Gutenberg's chief improvement:

recyclable letters known as movable type. Movable type consisted of individual letters made of metal that could be moved around and, therefore, could be completely reordered to form a brand new page. Setting the type for a page one tiny letter at a time might sound a bit tedious itself, but it was absolutely nothing compared to copying by hand or carving every individual letter in a woodblock. Once a page was set in movable type, the printer could print as many copies as he desired then simply move the letters around to print the next page of the book. Thus, on and on he could go, printing away page after page after clean, crisp, beautiful, new page. This was no mere improvement. This was a revolution.

A 1568 woodblock image of a printing press. The man on the left removes a finished page from the press while the one on the right inks the letters.

The individual metal letters were kept in big wooden trays where they were easily accessed by the typesetter as he put together a page of type. The capital letters were in one tray and the non-capitals, or little letters, in another. The little letters were used more often, so their tray, or case, was kept down low where it was slightly handier and easier to reach. The capital letters went in the upper, or higher, case. That's why capital letters are called *upper case* letters and small letters are *lower case*. The terms come from the early days of printing.

It became popular among the rich to talk about the latest book that had been published. They wanted books set out prominently in their houses, too, and, for the first time in over a thousand years, you were considered downright unfashionable if you could not read. So, the literacy rate skyrocketed. One of the first books printed by Gutenberg was a Bible, the standard Latin Vulgate edition. Known today as the Gutenberg Bible, it was the very first Bible in history to be put in print. Gutenberg did not pick the Bible to print because he was particularly religious, however. He did it because it was very good business. All the rich people wanted a copy—even though most of them couldn't read it since it was still in Latin.

The printing press had a seismic effect upon the whole culture of Europe. It was a central catalyst in both the Renaissance and the Protestant Reformation, two culture-shaping movements that mushroomed during the next century. The printing press, in fact, catapulted society into a whole new age, the Age of Print.

The Mystery of English Spelling

Remember the definition of a living language? It is one that is still being spoken somewhere and, therefore, changing. However, once a language is in print, the changes occur more slowly. But get this: bringing a language into print slows down changes in *spelling* more than changes in *pronunciation*. This seemingly insignificant detail is actually one of the chief culprits in making English so hard to spell.

Before the advent of print, there was no fixed, standard way to spell English words. Everyone pretty much spelled words however they said them. Pronunciations varied from one area to the next and this led to some interesting differences in spelling. Englishmen to the north put more Old Norse in their vocabulary and said things with an accent influenced by the Norse. Naturally, they would spell a word the way they said it. Englishmen to the west were influenced by the Celtic Welsh. They, too, spelled words the way they said them. But now, the abundance of print began to standardize spelling. But *whose* spelling should be used? Northumbrians and West Saxons were just two of several distinct dialects that existed in England at this time. So, which spelling should prevail? Simple. London's.

Spelling Caxton's Way

In 1476 William Caxton became the very first man to set up a printing press in England, and he put it in London, the capital city. London, where a central-southern dialect held sway, wielded the greatest influence on culture of any English city and, therefore, gave Caxton the greatest potential for selling what he printed. Viewed by many people as more sophisticated and educated, London dialect and spelling was simply smart for business. Thus, London dialect became the first standard for spelling

English words. No matter where you lived or how you pronounced your words, you spelled them as they did in London. This standardization of spelling was a process over a period of many years, but it wasn't long before the very new idea took shape in people's minds that there was a "right" and "wrong" way to spell words.

From Caxton's press in 1476 to our time, some pretty definite spelling changes have taken place, but spelling changes became like the slow movement of a glacier. In contrast, changes in pronunciation didn't slow down quite so much. Thus, we spell *knight* with that *k* and *gh* while no longer pronouncing those letters. The spelling of the word became standardized while pronunciation moved ahead.

English Spelling and the Great Vowel Shift

Coincidentally, as spelling changes slowed down, an unusually huge and fast shift in pronunciation began around this time. It started around 1400, the year Chaucer died, and about 50 years before Gutenberg's printing press. It is called the Great Vowel Shift and it is still going on to this day, though it has slowed down quite a bit.

Linguists argue over why the Great Vowel Shift even occurred. It's somewhat of a mystery. Most of the changes occurred in just one century, the 1400's, and by linguistic standards that is monumentally quick. As you can tell by its name, the shift was in the pronunciation of vowels. Long vowel sounds began to be made higher in the mouth (bet you never thought about where in your mouth you make your vowels), and the final *e* at the end of words became silent. *Lyf* (pronounced *leef*) became our *life*. *Doon* became our *down*. When you say those words, try to feel where you're forming them. You can tell that you are forming the first word of both pairs out near your teeth, and that the second, modern-day word feels like the vowel sound comes from farther back in your mouth.

By the time this Great Vowel Shift had made its most significant impact, much of our spelling had already been sent to the printer and was pretty much calcified. Many words were caught in pre-Great-Vowel-Shift form. When you add these vowel shifts together with all the other pronunciation changes, the ones that affected consonants, too, you've got a lot of words that today are not pronounced as they are spelled. The printing press was invented at the very end of the Middle Ages, and the Middle Ages is where much of our spelling remains.

So, now you know why English spelling can feel so unnatural at times, and, next time you have trouble spelling a word, you'll know who and what to blame—Gutenberg and the Great Vowel Shift.

✠✠✠ Æ ✠✠✠

Why, there isn't a man who doesn't have to throw out about fifteen hundred words a day when he writes his letters because he can't spell them!

Mark Twain

Famous American author,

who campaigned for the reform of English spelling.

Part IV

A Time of Transition—

From Middle to Modern English

1400 – 1600 (or thereabouts)

Around this time, two great whirlwinds of heart and mind grabbed Europe by the tail and slung around her greatest scholars and sculptors, painters and thinkers until they landed upright, gazing with new eyes at the future—because they'd had a life-changing new look at the past. The first movement was the Renaissance. It looked back to the past of the ancient Greeks and Romans as the great mass of all their scientific, mathematical and philosophical writings became available to Western Europe for the first time since the days of ancient Rome. And the second was the Reformation, which looked back at the ancient truths of scripture through the newly recovered lens of the Greek language.

So the last great language invasion was...can you guess? Greek! That is, Greek, along with even more Latin. Latin had never stopped oozing into English since Anglo-Saxon days. Now, the Renaissance and Reformation teamed up to ignite a kind of linguistic cannon stoked so full of Greek and Latin shot that the blast had enough new vocabulary to more than double the English dictionary.

The Invasion of Greek

Chapter 9

When I get a little money, I buy books,
and if any is left, I buy food and clothes.

Leonardo da Vinci
Renaissance artist, scientist, inventor

The Middle, the Modern, and the In-Between

Take a minute to look at your timeline in the front of the book as we review the dates for the Middle Ages. The Middle Ages extend from the fall of Rome, around 500 AD (476, to be exact) to around 1500 AD. They run from the *middle* of one millennium and continue to the *middle* of the next, though the term *Middle Ages* is actually derived from the fact that they are stuck in the middle between ancient and modern history. They represent a very long middle, too, a thousand years, a whole millennium of Middle Ages. Notice, though, there is an important break in the middle of that thousand-year period. The Battle of Hastings in 1066 separates the Early Middle Ages (or Dark Ages) from the Late Middle Ages. This break is especially significant for us as we study the history of our language because it separates Old English from Middle English. Then, the Modern Era goes from 1500 until the present day.

However, we didn't just hop from Middle Ages to Modern Times in one quick leap. As the timeline illustrates, there was a two-hundred-year transitional period overlapping the end of the Middle Ages and the beginning of modern times by around 100 years on either side. Historians argue over the precise dates, so these years are not exact, but we know that by 1400 when Chaucer died, a huge new movement was afoot. It swept first over Italy and then extended over all of Europe, lasting until around 1600, the time of William Shakespeare. Historians all agree that this special two hundred years marks a significant change in the cultural climate of all of Western Europe. It's as if a huge tidal wave of creative thinking hit the coast in Italy where it began, and the breakers kept on coming until the whole continent was awash with a new energy, a new excitement. This frothy tide of new intellectual and artistic ideas foamed and fermented all the way to the English Channel and across to the island kingdom of England. This period is known by the French word meaning "rebirth"—it is the *Renaissance*.

Rebirth of Ancient Knowledge

So what shook the cultural soda can to make all this bubbly fizz of discovery and creativity? Well, the most rigorous shake came from the re-discovery of the writings and teachings of the ancient Greeks and Romans. The scholars of the Middle Ages knew Latin, of course, but the study of many classical writers had been neglected during the Middle Ages, and as for the Greeks, knowledge of their language had been long gone from Western Europe. Thus, no one was able to study a Bible in the original Greek even if they'd had one, much less the other writings of the ancient Greek tradition. This was a real shame because among the ancient Greeks were scientists, artists, historians, and philosophers who had amassed a great deal of research and knowledge in their day. One reason the Dark Ages were "dark" is because all this knowledge had been lost with the collapse of the Roman Empire. Now the only Greeks who were studied were some whose works had been translated into Latin. Most of their research and scientific studies were unknown. The manuscripts were either unavailable or just forgotten, lying neglected in dark libraries of ancient monasteries. But it wouldn't have mattered anyway because in Western Europe no one could have read them since no one understood Greek.

Then during the Renaissance, a whole slew of ancient Greek writings became available, and Greek became part of the curriculum in western European universities. From the Sorbonne in Paris to England's Oxford University, ancient Greek documents were being studied and read in the original language for the very first time. Part of the reason for this turn-around in the study of ancient Greek manuscripts was that the Greek Byzantine Empire fell to the Muslim Turks. The *what* fell to *whom*? Let's back up a bit and let me explain what the Byzantine Empire was.

The Byzantine Empire

You know how we connected the beginning of the Middle Ages to the fall of the Roman Empire? Well, about a century before Rome actually fell, it split into two empires: a western half and an eastern half. The western half incorporated Italy and all those parts of Western Europe still under Rome's control. Its language was the language of Italy at that time—Latin. Because it included the city of *Rome*, it naturally retained the name *Roman* Empire.

The eastern half incorporated Greece and also cities that were Greek colonies in present day Turkey, and it included other territories, too, such as northeastern Africa, Israel, and more. Now get this, it was called the Roman Empire, too. Confusing? Very. So, in order to help clarify matters, historians have since conferred a distinct name on this eastern half of the Empire and it is now referred to as the Byzantine Empire. The name is derived from its capital city, Byzantium (later called Constantinople and, in modern times, Istanbul). In its day, this eastern empire was also sometimes simply called the "Empire of the Greeks" because its official language was Greek and most of its population was of Greek descent.

Therefore, when historians say that "the Roman Empire fell in 476 AD," they are actually talking about a reduced, diminished, western half, and not the former, gigantic, all-in-one-piece Roman Empire. So, what happened to this other half, the Greek Byzantine half? Well, it continued on for another *thousand* years. And along with it, there survived a Greek Church. That means that all during the Middle Ages, along with the Roman Catholic Church and its Latin language and traditions, there was also this other whole, huge Christian church known today as the Greek Orthodox Church. This Greek-speaking church grew directly from many of the Greek churches established by the Apostle Paul on his missionary journeys. Paul's letters to these churches make up most of our New Testament, so you already know the names of some of the eastern Roman Empire cities: Ephesus (Ephesians), Corinth (Corinthians), Thessalonica (Thessalonians), and Philippi (Philippians). After the Roman Empire split in two, all of these cities with their respective churches continued as part of the Byzantine Empire. So the Greek Church has a tradition just as rich and long-standing as the Catholic Church, and it was able to avoid some of the corruptions that festered within the Roman Catholic Church during the Middle Ages.

Re-Capturing Greek

It was the Muslim Turks who finally brought down the Byzantine Empire. By the time these Turks conquered Constantinople in 1453, crushing the empire for good, a lot of Greek-speaking, Greek Orthodox Christians had fled to Europe to escape the Muslim take-over. Some of the fleeing scholars began to teach in the universities in Western Europe, bringing their knowledge of the Greek language with them and introducing Greek into the curriculum for the first time. They also brought with them a cornucopia of ancient Greek literature, scientific writings, and...you should hear the sound of trumpets here...manuscript fragments of the New Testament *in Greek*. The Byzantine Church had preserved many New Testament documents in the original Greek, the language in which the New Testament was composed. These were still copies of the original writings, but they were not translations. Did you hear that? They were copies of the original writings in the original language, *not translations*.

It is because of the Greek manuscripts that became available at this time, along with a few that have been discovered in more recent centuries, that we can claim with such assurance that our modern translations of the Bible rest on a monumental degree of accuracy—far greater than any other ancient document. Now that is quite a claim. Let's look at why we Christians should feel confident to make it.

A Well-Documented Faith

There are three basic criteria upon which historians judge a piece of literature from ancient times. By "judge" I mean how do we really know that Homer's *Iliad* and *Odyssey* are actually what was written down by Homer around 800 BC? No one has an original copy. Or, how do we really know that our copies of Julius Caesar's *Gallic Wars* are actually what he wrote? Again, there's no original. Documents might get tampered with over time. They might be accidentally miss-copied, or get tweaked by well meaning scribes who have a personal agenda they wish to insert into the text. So how do we know if existing copies of an ancient document are true to the original? Here are the three primary factors used by experts to gauge reliability:

1.   The length of time between the date of the original writing and the date of the oldest copies.
2.   The number of copies that exist.

3. The degree to which the various copies agree with each other.

Take the *Iliad* for example. It is considered to be the best authenticated ancient document we have other than the New Testament. No one doubts that we have an accurate copy of this epic poem. So, let's look at the *Iliad* alongside Julius Caesar's *Gallic Wars,* Aristotle's writings, and the New Testament documents. They are listed in order of reliability.

Author	Date Written	Earliest Copy	Time span between original and oldest copy	Number of copies	Agreement among the copies
Julius Caesar	100-44 BC	900 AD	1000 yrs	10	-----
Aristotle	384-322 BC	1100 AD	1400 yrs	49	-----
Homer's *Iliad*	900 BC	400 BC	500 yrs	643	95 %
New Testament	50-100 AD	2nd Century	less than 100 yrs	5600	99.5%

Christian Apologetics and Research Ministry   http://www.carm.org

The oldest partial manuscripts of the New Testament are from as recent as fifty years after various books were written. The oldest complete New Testament dates from around 325 AD, and that's just 225 years after the original writing (compared to the Iliad's 2,000 years). And then we get to the number of copies or existing manuscripts, partial or complete. The number in the table above is only for ancient Greek manuscripts. There are over 10,000 more ancient Latin copies that are not even being counted above. Then add to that number the ancient Egyptian copies (Coptic manuscripts), plus various other copies that have been found of ancient origin, and you arrive at the incomparable number of *24,000 partial or complete ancient manuscripts.* These manuscripts have been meticulously compared and contrasted with each other to demonstrate beyond any reasonable doubt that what we have today is a thoroughly authenticated copy of the original writings.

None of this proves what the ancient manuscripts *claim.* But the first step must be to know for sure if these truly are the actual writings of the supposed authors. Then what they claim can be weighed and measured. Many people today have rejected Christianity because they think that the documents themselves are unreliable, that there are huge discrepancies in the texts, and that we don't actually know for sure what the early disciples wrote. That simply isn't true, and anyone who does some honest research will be confronted with the fact that we are in possession of a truly astounding quantity of reliable ancient manuscripts all of which attest to the accuracy of our New Testament. You can argue whether the events took place, but you just can't argue that these really are the writings of the men who claimed to have witnessed them.

Interestingly, the Roman Catholic Church preserved the greatest *number* of New Testament manuscripts, but the Greek Orthodox Church of the Byzantine Empire preserved the *oldest*. Makes sense when you think about it...the Greek speaking church saved the manuscripts that were written in Greek and, since the New Testament was originally composed in Greek, it follows that those would be some of the oldest texts.

All this Plus Print

Coincidentally, the Greek Empire fell just three years before Gutenberg opened up his printing shop in Germany and the printing press ushered the world into a new era. It wasn't long before print shops sprang up in many European cities and began pressing out a dazzling array of affordable books. Thus, the printing press became the great broadcaster of Renaissance ideas. Now Western Europe had Greek manuscripts, the knowledge to translate them, and the printing press to zip out multiple copies so they could be sent to universities, scholars, and curious commoners everywhere. It's no wonder we had a Renaissance!

Greek-Speak

At this time there was a huge influx of Greek words into the English language. Greek had always had a sort of back-door influence, anyway, through the Catholic Church and its Latin. During the era of the Roman Empire, Latin was the common tongue of Italy, but Greek was an international trade language. That's why the Gospel writers picked Greek for their New Testament writings. Latin adopted lots of words from Greek. So, Greek sneaked into our vocabulary from the beginning like a stowaway tucked inside the hull of Latin. But the majority of the words in our vocabulary today that are derived from Greek came in at the time of the Renaissance.

The Renaissance created a revolution in every field of human endeavor from physics, biology, and anatomy, to art, geography, and philosophy. Much of the advance in learning was spurred on by all the writings of the ancient Greek scientists and philosophers that were now available. That marvelous new invention, the printing press, was fueling the excitement by making books cheap and available. Greek words became popular. They were used to name all sorts of new things Europeans were learning and inventing. Just as Latin had always been (and would continue to be) a back up for labeling newly crystallized English ideas, now Greek words were being used the same way. Reshaping Greek words into modern English lingo became a virtual fad for those on the cutting edge of any endeavor. Anything new was labeled with Greek. In fact, Greek—and Latin, too—were used so much that some English writers accused others of grossly overusing Greek and Latin just in order to sound stylish and educated. Their words were dubbed "inkhorn words." An inkhorn was simply a bottle in which ink was kept, but an inkhorn *word* was a slur, insinuating that the words were being used merely to show off one's knowledge of Greek and Latin, not for any truly useful purpose. Of course, using foreign words to sound sophisticated was nothing new. Just a few centuries before, folks were throwing around as much French as possible in order to sound like the French-speaking upper class in England. Times change, but human nature doesn't.

From *video recorder* to *computer*, *megabyte* to *microwave*, our own era is still using Greek and Latin to coin new words for new things and new concepts. In fact, if you want to build your English vocabulary, just memorize the fifty or so most commonly used Greek and Latin root words. You will increase your ability to decipher unfamiliar English words, or at least make an educated guess at what they mean. Basically, because of the Renaissance, you can raise your SAT score by studying Greek and Latin roots. The word for *new word* itself is a Greek derivative: *neologism*. *Neo* means new, and *logos* means word. Look at the following Greek roots and notice how you can mix and match them:

photo = light	ology = study
mania = insanity	theos = God
graph = write	phobia = fear
bio = life	zoo = animals
auto = self	arachnid = spider

With the above definitions, you can see how English patched the following combos together:

photograph→ light writing
biology→ study of life
arachnophobia→ fear of spiders
theology→ study of God
biography→ writing the life [of someone]
autobiography→ writing the life of self
zoology→ study of animals
autograph→ writing self

And, of course, you can make up your own original (and crazy) neologisms such as: *zoomaniagraph*, someone who draws an insane amount of animal pictures; *autophobia*, the fear of having to do things by yourself; *arachnitheos*, the belief that spiders are gods (or that God is a spider?); and couldn't we call the Bible a *theography*?

The entrance of so much Greek during the Renaissance also explains some of the weirdest of our English spellings. These letter combos are almost always derived from Greek (the same way that the *sk* sound is a clue that a word is from Old Norse):

ph for the sound of *f* (photo, physical, philosophy)
ps for the sound of *s* (psychology, psychosis, psychic)
pn for *n* (pneumonia, pneumatic)
ch for the sound of *k* (Christ, charisma, character)

Also, every single English word that begins with an *x* is Greek in origin, except for *xanthic* which is French, and *X-ray*, a modern invention in which *X* just means unknown.

So, next time you hear someone say how strange it is that we don't just spell *photograph* with an *f*, you can tell them—it's Greek!

Life is pretty simple: You do some stuff.
Most fails. Some works.
You do more of what works.

Leonardo da Vinci
Renaissance artist, scientist, inventor

Sola Fide— A Battle Cry for Faith

Chapter 10

I cannot and will not recant anything,
for to go against conscience is neither right nor safe.
Here I stand, I can do no other, so help me God. Amen.

Martin Luther
Closing remarks at his trial before Catholic authorities.

While the Renaissance was gaining momentum throughout Europe, things were heating up on the religious front. A powerful movement, one that was both spiritual and political, broke forth in conjunction with the Renaissance. It was known as the Protestant Reformation. Like the Renaissance, the Reformation was jump-started by the rediscovery of Greek manuscripts and the introduction of the Greek language into universities in Western Europe. Christian scholars were hungry for knowledge of the Greek language so they could read the New Testament in its original language. They enthusiastically welcomed Greek scholars fleeing the Byzantine Empire to come teach Greek in the universities of England and Europe. Gradually the stage was set for the language-shaping, literature-lifting English Bible. So, let's focus briefly now on the Reformation and see what blessed havoc was wrought by a particular German scholar, a spunky monk named Martin.

Martin Luther

Martin Luther was a young German law student when one providential night a terrible storm came upon him while he was traveling from his parents' home back to the university. Bolts of lightning flashed all around him. Fearing he might be struck, he gave his life to God and promised to enter the Church instead of becoming a lawyer. He became a monk in the Augustinian Order and was eventually sent to the German town of Wittenberg to study, teach and preach. It was at this time that he began to study the New Testament for the first time in his life.

Martin Luther

Like Wycliffe before him, Luther began to see discrepancies between the official teachings of the church and what the Bible actually said. He, too, began to sense the urgent need for Bibles translated into the common languages of the people. In 1517, on the day we call Halloween, he nailed his Ninety-Five Theses (points of dispute), to the door of the church in Wittenberg. The church door acted as a public bulletin board in those days. He chose Halloween, or All Hallows Evening, because it was the day before All Hallows Day, which is now called All Saints Day. He knew everyone would be coming to the church the next morning for services on All Saints Day and, therefore, would see his document. Ironic, isn't it, that Luther did this on Halloween—the perfect time for spiritual warfare to begin. And warfare it was.

Since the printing press was around now, Luther wasn't hampered as Wycliffe had been with the slow labor of making hand copies. Instead, his writings, which soon included books and pamphlets, too, were printed up by the thousands and distributed all over Europe. So it wasn't long before Luther was in big trouble with the Church. He was finally brought to trial by a Roman Catholic council, declared a heretic, and excommunicated (barred from fellowship) by order of the pope. He would have been executed for heresy, but good friends conspired to help him escape, and he was whisked away to a castle to live in secret until his life was no longer in danger.

By this time Luther had a large following among the German people, and his break with the church fueled their discontent. News of his trial began to reach the ears of all of Europe, and the momentum of the Reformation could no longer be contained. Many people were eager to create a new church that would not be under the totalitarian reign of the pope.

They were hungry for grace and ready to be free of Roman Catholic corruption.

New churches began to form in the wake of Luther's teaching, and because these churches were *protesting* against the Catholic Church, the people who joined them were called *Protestants*. In fact, all the major Christian denominations that were founded at this time are still today, almost five hundred years later, referred to as Protestant churches. Presbyterian, Methodist, Baptist, and, of course, Lutheran, are among some of these mainstream Protestant denominations. And the movement as a whole was called the Protestant Reformation.

Purchasing Salvation—Hmmm. Didn't Jesus Already Do That?

A good bit of Protestant discontent simmered around a Catholic belief in a place called purgatory. According to Roman Catholic tradition, very few believers went straight to heaven when they died. Instead they went to purgatory where they could finish paying for their sins (as if Jesus' death were not quite payment enough). It was believed that once your departed spirit had suffered awhile in purgatory (a kind of quasi-hell), then and only then, were you allowed to go on to heaven. Discouraging thought, isn't it? But here's the worst part: The Catholic Church taught that if you paid money to the church by buying what was called an indulgence, you could shorten your time in purgatory or get out of it altogether, and you could even buy an indulgence for someone who was already dead in order to get them released. You were, at least in part, buying your salvation. An actual jingle used by the monk John Tetzel as he sold indulgences in Luther's day went like this:

"As soon as the coin in the coffer rings,
A soul from purgatory springs!"

The church hierarchy encouraged these beliefs in order to raise money. The church even put pressure on the very poor, who needed to spend their money for food and other necessities, to give their money to the church to buy indulgencies. The church played upon people's sympathy for dead relatives who might still be suffering in the afterlife. To top it off, the church was not using this money to build homeless shelters, stock food banks, or send out missionaries. Rather, it was used to buy land, build elaborate cathedrals, furnish lavish living situations for corrupt clergy, pay off public officials, support mistresses and their children (the pope of

Luther's day had three illegitimate children), and pay for all sorts of other not-so-righteous-things. No wonder many of these corrupt officials feared the thought of the common people being able to read the Bible for themselves. Heaven forbid that they should discover what it *really* said. Oh, no! The church might have to quit selling indulgences. Great Scot! Someone might even come to believe that we're saved by faith alone!

The battle cry of the Reformation came to rest on what Protestants believe to be two central truths of our faith, both of which blast away at the belief in purgatory and its accompanying practice of selling indulgences:

> (1) **Sola Scriptura**—a Latin phrase meaning "scripture alone." In other words, Christians should get their doctrine solely from the Bible (and not church traditions or the pope).

> (2) **Sola Fide**—a Latin phrase meaning "faith alone." Our good works, penances, or indulgences cannot be added to the work of Christ, and they can't buy salvation. What Jesus did on the cross was sufficient for the salvation and forgiveness of all believers. We are saved by "faith alone" and not as a result of works.

At this point, it is very important to note that the Catholic Church today is very different from the Church in the Middle Ages. The Catholic Church went through its own reformation a little later, the Counter Reformation, which involved a major cleaning out of old corruptions. Protestants still disagree with some significant Catholic doctrines, but Roman Catholic authorities today are as appalled as we are at these medieval scam artists in priests' robes. And remember, too, this was the Church of Augustine of Canterbury, Caedmon, the Venerable Bede, King Alfred, and many other faithful, loving, devout believers. Despite its corruptions, the Church sent forth the light of the gospel into many hearts. Luther declared that it was because of his *love* for the Church that he made his protest.

Now, can you guess what Martin Luther did first after he quit being a monk in the Catholic Church? He began translating the Bible into his native language, German, so Germans everywhere could start reading the truth for themselves. The second thing he did was to get married. He married a former nun and they had six children.

The End of the Middle

The invasion of Greek marks the last of our invasions of English. It also marks the end of the Middle Ages, the period that incorporated both Old English and Middle English. The Renaissance, with its re-introduction of the writings of ancient Greek philosophers and scientists, and the Reformation, with its emphasis on Greek manuscripts of the Bible, had teamed up to inject great gobs of Greek words into the English language. This double-barreled linguistic shotgun represents the peak of the Greek invasion of English, but the invasion is actually still going on today as we continue to adopt both Greek and Latin words to name our new ideas and inventions.

We have seen how corrupt and powerful forces were aligning themselves within the Roman Catholic Church of this time, forces aimed at stifling the truths of the Reformation and preventing Bibles from coming out in the common languages of the day. But the Reformation had too much momentum to be stopped now, and the fiery ambition to translate the Bible into all the spoken languages of Europe could not be doused. However, as we shall see in the next section, the struggle was especially intense and tragic over the translation of a Bible into English. So, next we turn to examine that particular wrestling match more closely, and we will see how and why the English Bible made such a deep and indelible impression on the shape and form of English.

✠✠✠ 𝔄𝔈 ✠✠✠

Pray, and let God worry.

Martin Luther

Part V

The Making of the English Bible

1526—1611

English had been belittled for centuries, even by Englishmen themselves. Indeed, how could it ever measure up to the scholarly precision of Latin or the literary elegance of French? But English was soon to shed the stigma of its years as an underling to both French and Latin, and through a very specific achievement, English would establish itself as an equal among all the great languages of the world, living or dead. That achievement was the English Bible—*in print*—especially the King James Version. We shall see how the English Bible would show the world that English could convey man's deepest yearnings and God's greatest truths with all the precision, depth, beauty and nuance of great literature. Those who had doubted the capabilities of English were silenced once and for all by this one achievement, and English would never again be seen as a second-rate language that was only suitable for grocery lists, bedtime stories and giving orders to your maid.

But just why was getting a Bible into English so difficult? After all, the printing press was around now, and Wycliffe had already made one English translation of the Bible, hadn't he? This should be a snap, right? Well, not quite.

English Contraband:
Fulfilling Wycliffe's Dream

Chapter 11

Contrary to what history teaches about Chaucer being the father
of the English Language, this mantle belongs to William Tyndale,
whose work was read by ten thousand times as many people as Chaucer.

From a museum exhibit co-sponsored by the British Library
and the Library of Congress

www.williamtyndale.com

Outlawing English

You may recall that after Wycliffe's death, the prospects for getting
a Bible in English actually got worse. The Bibles he and his followers had
translated and hand-copied into English were confiscated and burned. The
English clergy and government officials were growing even more fearful of
rebellions, and in many of their minds the rebellions were connected to
Reformation ideas. These fears were not without reason. Some of the more
radical-minded of the reform preachers encouraged the common people to
rise up and take by force all the lands and houses from wealthy church
officials. Peasants were revolting in many parts of Europe, and they readily
quoted Reformation leaders to defend their violent causes. Reformers like
Martin Luther were distressed that the rediscovered truths of the Reformation were being misused by these radical political factions. Certainly, the
dangers were real – on both sides.

In 1381 there was a massive revolt in England. Thirty thousand ri-
oting peasants descended on London to protest a new tax. Thousands were
killed during the rebellion. Many were executed afterwards. The leaders of
this rebellion claimed to be following Wycliffe as they pointed out the
rampant greed of those in authority. They blamed the wealthy, land-

holding Catholic Church and clergy for much of their suffering. So the clergy had reason to fear Reformation ideas, and it seemed to many that making Bibles available in the common person's language fueled these new beliefs. Indeed, what effect would a Bible in English have? It might empower the peasants even more.

In 1407 the archbishop of Canterbury ruled:

> We therefore legislate and ordain that nobody shall from this day forth translate any text of Holy Scripture on his own authority into the English, or any other language, whether in the form of a book, pamphlet or tract...whether composed recently or in the time of John Wycliffe, or in the future, shall not be read in part or in whole, in public or in private.

Quoted in Allister McGrath's *In The Beginning*

What had been discouraged was now out-and-out illegal. For the first time in history, *any* scripture in English was totally banned.

Henry VIII 1491—1547

Enter Henry VIII

A little more than a hundred years after the above proclamation, the Reformation was in full swing in many parts of Europe. England, by contrast, was busy having public burnings of Luther's books. The country remained stubbornly determined to staunch the flow of Reformation ideas, and any scripture in English was still a capital offense.

The king of England at this time was a heavy-set outdoorsman who loved hunting and jousting, had a keen wit, and enjoyed hosting boisterous royal parties to entertain his court. His name was Henry VIII, and he was, for the time being, married to a devout Catholic woman.

In the year of 1526, Henry was greatly startled and perturbed one day to hear that there were copies of the complete New Testament in English being circulated in London. How could that be? Where did they come from? Who had printed them? Who translated them? Henry wanted to know; he wanted to bury the guy who did it. There was absolutely no information on the title page where the author and printer were usually named. It would take some investigating to find out who was behind it.

It was obvious these New Testaments had not been printed in England. The printing houses were well known, and it would have been impossible to print such a large order on a long book without detection. It must be that they were being smuggled in from somewhere in Europe. When I think of smuggling, I think of heroin or cocaine— illegal and dangerous substances. Or, I think of Brother Andrew smuggling Bibles into communist Russia, or missionaries who smuggle them into Red China today. Isn't it ironic that New Testaments in English had to be smuggled into Christian England simply because they were *in English*? Dangerous contraband, indeed.

Scriptures for a Ploughboy

Some people are born with a particular genius for languages. Remember Sir William Jones? He was fluent in many languages at an early age and ended up discovering the connection between English and Ancient Sanskrit. Or, take Champollion, a Frenchman who could read and write Hebrew, Arabic, Syriac, Chaldean and Chinese by the age of ten. In the early 1800's he discovered the key to translating ancient Egyptian hieroglyphs. We take for granted all the history we now know about ancient Egypt, but we didn't have that knowledge until Champollion translated the Rosetta Stone so hieroglyphs could finally be deciphered.

A man named William Tyndale was also one who had a special gift for languages. Tyndale grew up in England, attended Oxford University, and was ordained as a priest in the Catholic Church, which, of course, was still the only church in England. During that time he had gained a reputation among his professors and peers for being especially sharp at languages. He was fluent in eight languages including Greek, which had been introduced into the curriculum at Oxford during the Renaissance. But more important than any of this, William Tyndale had become ignited with the same fire as Wycliffe: the burning desire to get the Bible to the English people in their own language. During his years at Oxford, Tyndale had become wholeheartedly converted to the ideas of the Reformation and to the liberating truths of *Sola Fide* and *Sola Scriptura*. Now, he wanted to share these truths with his fellow countrymen. He wanted to see the English people freed from the burdens of legalism (thinking you had to earn salvation) and released from the lies of a corrupt church. Tyndale knew that the truth would spread on its own if he could just get them a Bible they could read, so he began working on an English translation of the New Testament. When a fellow cleric in the church criticized him for this endeavor, Tyndale responded, "If God spare my life, ere many years I will cause a boy that driveth the plough shall know more of the Scriptures than thou doest." A common ploughboy reading and understanding the Word of God? No doubt the cleric merely laughed.

There was no printer in England at this time who could take the considerable risk to print illegal English Bibles. Actually, it wasn't just risky, it was pure suicide. So, Tyndale sailed for Europe and began lining up someone to put his translation into print. Between Catholic authorities after him for heresy, and the henchmen of Henry VIII who would arrest anyone trying to produce an English Bible, he had to take great efforts to keep his whereabouts a secret. But he managed to finish a printing of the New Testament in 1526 (at the age of 32), and it was immediately smuggled into England. It was the very first pocket-sized Bible, and those favoring Protestant ideas circulated it with great enthusiasm.

But money to fund the printings was sometimes hard to come by. Alister McGrath, in his book *In The Beginning*, tells the story of Bishop Tunstall of England who had gone to Europe to hunt down Tyndale's Bibles in order to have them destroyed. When Tunstall happened upon someone who knew where to buy them in large quantity, he purchased as many as possible and immediately had the books burned. However, the seller was actually a friend of Tyndale, and even though these books were destroyed, Tyndale was delighted to make such a quick and generous profit. The money was enough to print an entire new edition. Tunstall had unwittingly subsidized the production of the very books he was determined to stamp out.

Tyndale eventually settled down in Antwerp, Belgium, a publishing center for much of Europe. Antwerp was dangerous because it was very near Brussels, a city that was staunchly Roman Catholic. But Tyndale lived with friends who kept his identity a secret, and with the New Testament now completed and being smuggled into homes all over England, he turned to translating the Pentateuch, the first five books of the Old Testament.

Erasmus

As you may recall, Wycliffe's edition of the English Bible had been a translation from the Latin Vulgate Bible because that was the only version available to him. But by Tyndale's time, the Renaissance scholar Desiderius Erasmus had put together a complete Greek and Latin New Testament. The scripture for the book was printed in two columns with the Greek on the left and the new Latin translation on the right. Scholars were excited about having a fresh Latin translation, but this was nothing compared to having the very first complete New Testament *in Greek*, the language in which the New Testament was originally written.

Martin Luther used Erasmus' landmark Greek New Testament as his primary text to make his German translation. Now, Tyndale also used Erasmus' text to produce his English edition. Tyndale's New Testament was the first *printed* New Testament in English, but more importantly, it was *the very first English New Testament to be translated from the original Greek.*

With Erasmus' Greek New Testament available now, and men like Luther and Tyndale working to get the Word into the common languages, the Bible was no longer locked away in Latin—and it never would be again. The era of the open Bible had begun.

Translation Trailblazing

The work of a translator is always tricky. Translating into English, a language that had undergone huge increases in vocabulary, meant that for every word in Greek or Hebrew there might be as many as half a dozen in English from which to choose. The translator must choose the one word most fitting, most precise, and the one that best typifies the style of the original writer. Not only that, but translation of complex concepts sometimes involves the invention of brand new words and phrases—ways of saying things that would fasten themselves forever in the hearts and minds of all English speaking Christians. In other words, the very first Bible to be printed and made available in English would likely have an enduring effect. All English translations to follow would make use of this first one and would in some way reflect it.

Tyndale was primarily concerned with clarity and accuracy of translation, but he definitely aimed at beauty, too, and he possessed a natural talent for feeling the rhythm of speech. He was good at creating memorable phrases that would roll off your tongue and stick in your head. Much of the beauty of the later and better-known King James Version of the Bible comes directly from Tyndale. In fact, in recent years, because of the precision of computer analysis, scholars have begun to understand the full extent to which Tyndale's translation actually ended up in the King James Bible. Analysts now say as much as 80% of the entire King James Bible is pure Tyndale, and the King James Version New Testament is fully 90% the work of this one man.

Tyndale's Word Choices

Tyndale leaned heavily toward using Anglo-Saxon derived words. Now, what difference does that make, you may ask? Well, the words we've adopted from the Latin and French tend to be more sophisticated, cultured and polysyllabic (having more than one syllable). This is a generalization and there are exceptions, of course, but overall the most simple, basic words in our vocabulary tend to be Anglo-Saxon. Of the 100 most often used words in English, all are Anglo-Saxon. All are one syllable, too. If you write a paragraph and use only one-syllable words, you'll dramatically increase the percentage of pure Anglo-Saxon you are using. In fact, it can also increase the power and punch of your writing. That's a good thing to remember when you're writing your next essay for a class. Without question, students should work to increase their vocabulary. The more words you have from which to choose, the richer and more precise will be your choices. However, using more Anglo-Saxon can give a story or essay a kind of stripped-down straightforwardness that it might not have otherwise. If you're aiming at rugged and simple, as opposed to flowery and ornate, go with the Anglo-Saxon.

So, going for the long, educated-sounding word is not always synonymous with good writing, and William Tyndale knew that. He was keen on being simple, clear, and direct. Listen to the short words from Tyndale's Genesis 1:

Then God said: Let there be light and there was light.
And God saw the light that it was good.

He did <u>not</u> say:

Let there be illumination. And God perceived that the illumination was beneficial.

Tyndale's Inventions

Tyndale had to do some inventing, too. He needed some new English words to convey a few things never verbalized before in English. Some of his words became standard to Christian speech. He coined the English words *Passover, atonement,* and *scapegoat.* And, everyone knows the term *Jehovah* for the name of God. That was Tyndale's construction for God's name from the Hebrew.

Same thing goes for many of Tyndale's phrases. These are familiar to us because they were incorporated into the King James Version, but each one is a Tyndale original.

- Let there be light
- Eat, drink and be merry
- The powers that be
- A prophet has no honor in his own country
- Fight the good fight
- Am I my brother's keeper?
- The salt of the earth
- In him we live and move and have our being
- A man after His own heart
- Sign of the times
- It came to pass
- Gave up the ghost
- A law unto themselves
- Ask, and it shall be given you; seek and ye shall find
- The spirit is willing but the flesh is weak
- For unto you is born this day in the city of David, a saviour which is Christ the Lord [And 98% of the rest of Luke 2—the classic Christmas story]

[From www.williamtyndale.com and www.tyndale.org]

If these phrases sound familiar, it is not just because you've heard them in the Bible. When words or sayings or phrases become deeply embedded in the mind of a whole culture, they pop up everywhere, from book titles, to songs, to side references in articles and short stories, to everyday speech. They become idioms in our speech, used over and over in a multitude of ways. Those who don't know the Bible at all use them, unaware of their origin, thinking of them as mere cultural expressions.

Translating the Bible—A Political Activity?

Besides simple clarity, precise handling of the Greek had political ramifications. Tyndale always tried to choose the most straightforward rendering of the Greek, but that had a natural tendency to back up Reformation thinking. The Roman Catholic Church did not like his choices at all.

For instance, Tyndale took the Greek word *ekklesia,* which literally means *an assembly*, and translated it as *congregation*. The Catholic Church wanted it to be translated *church*, a word that would put more weight on the church as an institution, rather than on the people themselves as the body of Christ. One little word...but it made a big difference.

Then there was the Greek word *presbyteros*. Tyndale went with the English word *elder* instead of the Catholic preference *priest*. Another "hot" word was the Greek *metanoia*, which Tyndale translated *repent*. In the Greek it literally means *a change of mind*. The Catholic Church, however, preferred the English word *penance*, a traditional Roman Catholic concept that involved a type of compensation given for one's sins by an act of kindness, self-denial, or even payment of money to the church. A simple matter of translating one word, but it had the power to affect one's understanding of Jesus' death on the cross. Had his death completely paid for our sins or not? Do we give to the church out of gratefulness for Christ's payment, or because we need to *add* to His payment for our sins? So, now, see if you can pick out which one of the translations below is from a Bible version popular among Roman Catholics:

Repent, for the kingdom of heaven is at hand! —*King James Version*
Do penance: for the kingdom of heaven is at hand. —*Douay-Rheims*
Repent, for the kingdom of heaven is near. —*NIV*
Change your life. God's kingdom is here. —*The Message*

--Matthew 3:2

You probably easily picked out the Douay-Rheims Bible. Notice, too, how closely the others agree in content though they are different in style. There is such thorough agreement among the other versions that you can be sure you're getting an accurate translation. Today, we take for granted this host of different versions of the Bible available to us. But these versions are an important protection against the misuse and abuse of a translation being slanted toward one particular group's special interests or beliefs. One denomination can't "con" us about what a particular word or verse is saying because we can compare and contrast different translations for ourselves and make up our own minds. With one click on the computer, we can go to the Internet and get numerous English translations of any passage of scripture we wish to study. Tyndale wanted people to have this kind of option. He would have loved seeing all the Bibles we have today and all of us "ploughboys" studying the Bible for ourselves.

✠✠✠ Æ ✠✠✠

Because someone has the gift of languages and understands them,
that does not enable him to turn one into the other and to translate well.
Translating is a special grace and gift of God.

Martin Luther

Of Kings and Wives and Martyrs

Chapter 12

*A*s the holly groweth green
And never changeth hue,
So I am, and ever hath been,
Unto my lady true.

Original verse by King Henry VIII
www.luminarium.org

Obsession For a Son

Henry VIII was married to a devout Catholic, Catherine of Aragon. He grew increasingly displeased with her because she had not given him a son. Catherine had lost several babies and had given Henry only one child who survived, a girl named Mary. In Henry's mind, it was having a male heir to the throne that kept the country's government stable and out of civil war. It is true that civil wars are sometimes the outcome of a king's death when only cousins and nephews are left to vie for the throne. Having a direct male descendent certainly cuts out any confusion. But Henry's desire was a total obsession, defining his life. It ended up bringing much misery to Henry himself as well as to his country, not to mention his wives. Above all, it ended up being one of history's great ironies, because the monarch who is celebrated as being one of the greatest, wisest, and most popular in all of English history is Queen Elizabeth I, one of Henry's *daughters*.

When a Powerful King Wants an Unobtainable Divorce

Henry made up his mind to divorce Catherine. He had already fallen in love with another woman, Anne Boleyn, and she had become pregnant with Henry's child. (These people really needed a Bible they could read!) Henry just knew he was about to have the son he always wanted, and, if he could just obtain a divorce from Catherine and marry Anne, the child would be in line to inherit the throne. Now, you must realize, a divorce was not easy to obtain within the Roman Catholic Church. It required a special dispensation, or legal exemption, issued by the pope. But the popes were often doing things for political reasons (the church was corrupt, remember), and so Henry petitioned the pope to have his marriage annulled (a particular variety of divorce). Under normal circumstances, the divorce would probably have been granted. However, Catherine, who was very unhappy about Henry's attempt to divorce her, just happened to be kin to the Holy Roman Emperor Charles V whose army was threatening the pope at this time. The pope refused to grant the divorce because he didn't want to make Charles V any madder than he already was.

So Henry came up with an outlandishly bold, creative alternative. Henry decided to force Parliament—the British version of our Congress—into legally separating the English church from the Roman Catholic Church just so he could get a divorce. England divorced the pope, you might say, in order for Henry to divorce Catherine. When the English government officially declared it was splitting with Rome, the Archbishop of Canterbury was free to grant the divorce, which he swiftly did. Henry married Anne immediately. The pope, in turn, immediately excommunicated Henry from the Catholic Church. Of course, Henry didn't mind that at all. He was finally happy. He sat back and relished his new position as the supreme head of something that had never before existed in all of history: an independent Church of England.

Heads Begin to Roll

Not everyone went along with Henry, of course. There were lots of faithful Catholics in England to whom this was just plain heresy. Many were deeply upset, but only two churchmen, Thomas More and John Fisher, refused to sign the papers making Henry head of the church in England instead of the pope. Eventually, though both of these men had been faithful subjects and good friends to Henry, Henry had them both arrested and then beheaded. Henry the VIII had few scruples about executing friends...or wives, as we shall see.

The Church of England, for the time being at least, remained completely Catholic in its form of worship and beliefs—except, of course, there was no pope now, just Henry. Those who were in agreement with the ideas of the Reformation were jubilant. How wonderful! Finally, England had her own separate church, and perhaps over time England would become more and more Protestant. Perhaps it would be easier to reform an English Church than a Roman Catholic one. And the good news just kept on coming, for as it turned out, Anne Boleyn was very sympathetic to Protestant ideas. Surely, she would have great influence upon King Henry...wouldn't she?

The 1534 Convocation of Canterbury

In 1534, the year after Henry wed Anne Boleyn, there was a meeting of officials in the Church of England called the Convocation of Canterbury. The Convocation petitioned King Henry to issue an official, legal Bible in the English language. It had proved impossible to stop Tyndale's New Testament, and the whole matter was becoming an embarrassment to the government and to the clergy, too. It was pretty obvious that the English people were going to have an English Bible one way or another, legal or illegal.

However, because Tyndale and his translation had become so closely associated with extreme Protestant views, it was agreed they must wait on another Bible for the king to sanction. But it was a done deal now, and the matter settled at last. The people of England would have their English Bible, legal to own and officially sanctioned.

A Prayer for the King

Meanwhile, Tyndale was living with friends in Antwerp, Belgium, under an assumed name. Then, just a few months after the Convocation of Canterbury, right when the political climate in England had finally warmed-up to an English Bible, a trusted acquaintance of William Tyndale betrayed him to the Catholic authorities. He was arrested in Antwerp for heresy against the Roman Catholic Church. He was held prisoner in a cold, dilapidated, two-hundred-year-old castle for almost a year and a half. Some historians speculate that Henry VIII might have been able to secure his release. However, Tyndale had openly opposed Henry's divorce and marriage to Anne on the grounds that it was not scriptural, and, on top of that, Henry was much distracted by other matters by this time.

Henry's wife Anne Boleyn had fallen out of favor with him. First, she had given birth to a girl (the future Queen Elizabeth I), and then had delivered a child that was stillborn. She had not given Henry the hoped-for male heir. Now, another woman of the court had caught Henry's eye, a young woman he thought could surely bear him sons. Of course, that's just what he'd thought about Anne. But Henry, once again, was determined to get his way. He instigated the filing of criminal charges against Anne, accusing her of adultery. Though no evidence was ever produced to confirm Henry's accusations, she was put into prison in the Tower of London, brought to trial under those charges, and beheaded in May of 1536. If Anne had still been in a position of influence, she might have persuaded the King to do something to help Tyndale. Anne even owned a Tyndale New Testament that she kept on her bedside table (on display today in the Library of London). But now, Henry wanted nothing to do with helping a Protestant heretic.

About six months after Anne's execution, in October of 1536, William Tyndale was tied to a wooden stake with kindling piled around his feet ready to be lit. A large crowd had gathered to watch. As an act of mercy, a rope was tied around his neck and he was strangled first, then his body burned at the stake. It is recorded that just before the execution he shouted out his last words so everyone could hear, and his words were repeated all over England as the story of his execution spread: "Lord, open the king of England's eyes!"

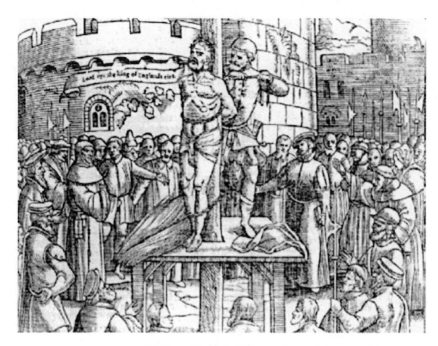

William Tyndale's Execution
A woodcut image from an early edition of *Foxe's Book of Martyrs*.

Faith

Faith is then a lively and a steadfast trust in the favor of God...
and such trust, wrought by the Holy Ghost through faith,
maketh a man glad, lusty, cheerful, and truehearted unto God
and unto all creatures: whereof, willingly and without compul-
sion, he is glad and ready to do good to every man, to do service
to every man, to suffer all things, that God may be loved and
praised, which hath given him such grace; so that it is impossible to separate good works from faith, even as it is impossible
to separate heat and burning from fire.

William Tyndale

From his prologue to the Book of Romans

The Bible That Was Named for a King

Chapter 13

> Now what can bee more auaileavle thereto, then to deliuer Gods booke
> vnto Gods people in a tongue which they vnderstand?

Preface, Holy Bible, King James Version 1611

[Note the "u" and "v" which were not separate letters at this time
and were printed interchangeably]

The Geneva Bible

Just one year after Tyndale's execution, the first complete Bible in English came out in print, the Coverdale Bible. It was followed by a succession of English Bibles, all legal, which became popular and readily available to the English people. All made use of William Tyndale's translation. Of these various Bibles, by far the most popular was the Geneva Bible, the first "study Bible" in English. Though other Bibles had some marginal notes and commentary (better known among literary types as *glosses*), the Geneva Bible was the first Bible to contain extensive commentary. Most historians think that it is also the Bible from which Shakespeare quoted whenever he used Bible references in his plays.

A Succession of Monarchs

In 1547, while on wife number six, Henry VIII died. For the next 56 years of England's history, one of Henry's children was on the throne in the following order:

(1) Edward VI, Henry's only son (by third-wife Jane Seymore), was crowned at the age of nine in 1547. He died just six years later.

(2) Mary I was crowned in 1553. She was Henry's daughter by his first wife, the devout Catholic, Catherine of Aragon. Mary was

also called "Bloody Mary" because she burned so many Protestants at the stake in a futile attempt to make England a Roman Catholic country again.

(3) Elizabeth, Henry's daughter by the ill-fated Anne Boleyn, became Queen Elizabeth I in 1558.

Queen Elizabeth I ended up being one of the most respected and admired monarchs of all time. She had a long reign of almost 45 years. Following her Catholic sister Mary to the throne, Elizabeth reinstated the

Elizabeth I of England

Church of England and returned England to a more Protestant faith. Elizabeth's name also became synonymous with the language spoken in her day. Though technically the English of that time is considered to be the beginning of modern English, it obviously differs from our own. It is the English of William Shakespeare and the King James Bible. It is commonly called Elizabethan English.

Elizabeth was known as the Virgin Queen because she never married and our state of Virginia is named for her. When she died, she left no direct descendant to inherit the throne, so a request was sent to her cousin James VI of Scotland to take the English throne. In this way, England hoped to finally unite the two countries of Scotland and England in the deal as well. James consented and became...

James I of England

As King James I of England, he remained James VI of Scotland. After centuries of fighting between the Scots and the English, James' coronation officially joined these two countries under one government without any bloodshed. This was nothing short of astounding. The term *Great Britain* was used for the very first time during his reign to refer to both these newly united countries, though the title was not official until later. So after 1100 years, England was called *Britain* once again—just like in Roman times. King James was the first king in over half a century who was *not* a child of King Henry VIII.

When James I came to the throne, England was still very much divided in its religious loyalties. There were many staunch Catholics in England still, as well as reform-minded Protestants. James wanted to soothe the sharp divisions between them and thought that a new official Bible might help. He felt that the Geneva Bible, the most popular at that time, was too divisive because its commentary and notes were so blatantly Protestant. Historians agree that the notes were, indeed, intensely anti-Catholic.

James VI of Scotland
James I of England

So James was struggling for a middle ground, as were many mainstream Christians in the Church of England at that time. On one side, there were those still faithful to their Catholic roots. On the other side there was a growing and highly vocal group of Puritans. These "Puritan pests," as King James once called them, were viewed as being on the radical side of Protestant. Some were even Presbyterian. Oh, my! Being Presbyterian, in many people's minds, was equivalent to wanting to get rid of the monarchy and install a republican form of government. Presbyterianism is a republican form of church government, and many Presbyterians actually did very much want to extend this type of government to the country itself. King James had run into many of these types in his native country, Scotland, which was a virtual breeding ground for rabid Presbyterians.

So, the primary reason King James wanted a new Bible was to get a translation that would be acceptable to a broad variety of English folks. He desired two things:

(1) A Bible translation that was not too Protestant and not too Catholic with which everyone could be happy.

(2) A Bible that had no commentary of any kind.

James' great hope was that this Bible might be a unifying force for all of Great Britain. And, indeed, that's exactly what it proved to be.

The Apocrypha

James commissioned a committee of fifty-four scholars to work on the new translation. All other English Bibles were used for comparison. The translators were divided into three large groups to translate the three basic sections of the Bible to be included. *"Three* sections?" you may ask. You probably thought the Bible was in just two sections—Old Testament and New Testament. Not at this time. The three sections were the Old Testament, the Apocrypha, and the New Testament. The Apocrypha consisted of those books written by the Jews during the four hundred years that elapsed from the end of the Old Testament to the beginning of the New. Roman Catholics considered the Apocrypha to be on par with the rest of scripture. The Church of England did not. But it was traditional to include them, and it helped appease those who still leaned toward Catholicism. It made the Bible much bulkier, however, as well as more costly to print, and the Apocrypha was eventually dropped. Surprisingly, it was not officially removed until 1885, though many editions were printed without it before that year.

Southern Dialect Wins Again

The scholars on the translation team were connected to England's three leading universities: Oxford, Cambridge, and Westminster. It so happened, they were all men who had grown up in the lower mid-eastern to southeastern parts of England. This was basically the area around London. So, just as Caxton's printing press in London over a century earlier had made the London dialect the standard to follow in both spelling and vocabulary, now the King James Bible profoundly broadened that influence. Thus, the London dialect trumped the others for all time here because whatever English ended up being used in THIS book was going to be the English most widely read of any English out there anywhere...ever.

The image on the right is the title page to the first edition of the 1611 King James Bible, or Authorized Version, as it was often called. Apostles Peter and Paul are seated at the top in the center. Lower down, on either side of the text, are Moses and Aaron with Moses holding the tablets of the Law. The gospel writers, Matthew, Mark, Luke and John, sit in the four corners and the rest of the Apostles are gathered around Peter and Paul at the top.

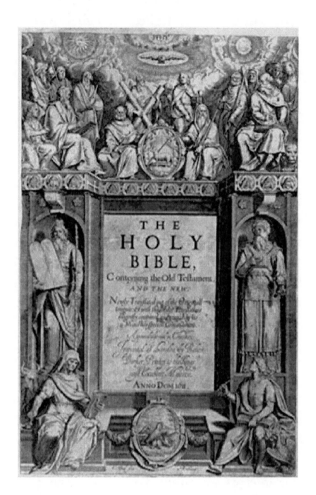

The English Civil War and the Bible

When the King James Bible made its debut in the year 1611, it was not immediately successful with the public. Puritan-leaning Christians still preferred the Geneva Bible with its Protestant notes for at least another generation. But, you know how wars affect things? Well, England had a civil war. During this war the Puritans actually took control of the government for a time. The king, James' son Charles I, was executed, and a Puritan Commonwealth replaced the monarchy for a little more than a decade. When the monarchy was finally restored in 1660, everyone was sort of tired of Puritans. The majority of English people just wanted to get things back to order. The popularity of the distinctively Protestant Geneva Bible faded, and from this point on, the King James Bible reigned supreme. In the English people's mind, the King James Bible supported the whole idea of having a king. After all, it was named for one.

America and The King James Bible

What English Bible was the first to be brought to America? We don't know for sure. Some historians say the best bet is the Bishops' Bible. Whatever it was, it wasn't the King James Version. There had already been two English settlements before the King James Bible was even printed: (1) The English settlement of Roanoke in which all the settlers mysteriously disappeared, and (2) Jamestown (also named for King James) in 1607. Considering the fact that these early settlers were risking their lives on a dangerous voyage into the unknown, they probably took along their Bibles. But it would have been one of the earlier versions. Next, after Jamestown, came the colony of Plymouth in 1620. Late enough for the King James Bible but consisting mainly of Pilgrims, the radicals among the Puritans, or the radical of the radicals, so to speak. They would most likely have had the Geneva Bible with them.

But it wasn't too long before the King James Bible took over in the American colonies—even among the Puritans—and the King James Bible was the first English Bible to be printed in America (1782). Was it the first Bible to be printed in America? No. The first printed Bible in North America was not in English at all, but in Algonquian, a Native American language. It was printed in 1663 and translated by John Eliot as part of his missionary effort to the Algonquian tribes.

Euphemisms and Shifting Sensibilities

It would shock some people to know there's at least one expression in the King James Bible of 1611 that today would be considered too crude to be in the Bible. We tend to think of those who lived in the past as being more prudish than we modern people are, but that is far from the truth. The King James Bible, like Chaucer and Shakespeare and others, was actually the product of a pretty open society when it came to body parts and the bodily functions of those parts. It was the later Victorian era, named for England's Queen Victoria, that took such an extremely prudish turn. Our own modern era has broken free from that, not always in a healthy fashion, of course. But still, you wouldn't want to go back to

Victorian times when some people actually thought you shouldn't even see yourself naked. Thin garments were worn in the bathtub by some young ladies to prevent such immodesty. Now *that* was prudish.

When sensibilities shift over a word or expression, we often substitute a euphemism to replace it. A euphemism is a polite term that we substitute for a harsh or crude term. For instance,

> *mentally challenged*—instead of *retarded*
>
> *passed away*—instead of *dead*
>
> *disabled*—instead of *paralyzed*

These are all euphemisms and we use them often out of sensitivity or social custom. For instance, we would never say we had a pet *killed* or *exterminated*. We say we "had it put to sleep." When I was growing up, it was considered improper to say that a woman was *pregnant*. You used a euphemism instead, saying simply, "She's going to have a baby." It meant the same thing, of course, but it had a softer, more polite sound to it. The word *pregnant* has since shifted and gone from unacceptable to acceptable. A euphemism is no longer used. One of the interesting ways in which all languages change is when words or expressions shift from being crude to being acceptable and vice versa.

A good example is in the 1611 King James Old Testament with its use of the word *piss*. *Piss* is a noun and is equivalent to our word *urine*. *Piss* is in there twice, and *pisseth* five times. *Pisseth* is the verb form—sounds like a joke doesn't it? In 1611, *piss* wasn't just spoken anywhere at anytime, but it was not considered crude either. It was just descriptive. Its use in the Bible comes from the Hebrew idiom to designate men as opposed to women by referring to those "who can piss against the wall." Since females don't have the necessary apparatus for accomplishing that feat, that became a Hebrew way to say "all you guys." Obviously, those Hebrews weren't too prudish either. Go to II Kings 9:8 for one example of this usage and see how your Bible translates it. Chances are it just says "males" and perhaps gives a notation in the margin saying how the Hebrew actually reads (my New American Standard did that).

Whacky but True: Shakespeare in a Psalm

There was only one other influence at this time that even came close to the King James Bible, and, of course, that was the incomparable playwright William Shakespeare. If you can memorize the year the King

James Version came out – 1611 – you will also have memorized a good generalized date for the time of Shakespeare, though this is near the end of his life. He was writing during the reign of both Queen Elizabeth and King James. There is no historical evidence at all that William Shakespeare had anything to do with the editing or translating work of the King James Bible. But there is a very odd and funny coincidence about the two of them. No one knows who first discovered this, or how in the world anyone could have found it, but it's as if a funny quirk of fate left Shakespeare's mark on the King James Bible.

If you take the year when the King James Version was being translated, 1610, and look up Shakespeare's age at that time, you'll find that he would have been 46 years old. Then go to the center of the Bible—Psalms— and go to the 46th Psalm. Next, count down to the 46th word of that Psalm and you'll find the word *shake*. Then, count up from the bottom (excluding the Hebrew term *selah*) to the 46th word from the end and you'll find the word *speare*. Shakespeare!

Richard Lederer in his book *Crazy English* has this to say about it: "Whether the embedded *shake spear* is a purposeful plant or the product of happy chance, the name of the world's most famous poet reposes cunningly in the text of the world's most famous translation." Lederer goes on to suggest that perhaps the translator of that passage was enjoying the playful placing of a secret tribute to his favorite playwright. By the year 1610, Shakespeare was already fabulously famous and receiving critical acclaim. Interestingly, Shakespeare at this time was one of the King's Players, the group designated to perform for the King. Could King James himself have orchestrated this crafty planting of words for his favorite playwright? We shall never know.

For your entertainment, I've included a copy of the 1611 King James Version of Psalm 46. I figured you might like to find *shake-speare* for yourself. I have reproduced it here with the original spellings and kept it as close as possible to the look of the original print-type.

PSAL. XLVI

God is our refuge and strength: a very present helpe in trouble.

2 Therfore will not we feare, though the earth be remoued: and though the mountaines be caried into the midst of the sea.

3 Though the waters thereof roare, and be troubled, though the mountaines shake with the swelling thereof. Selah.

4 There is a riuer, the streames wherof shall make glad the citie of God: the holy place of the Tabernacles of the most High.

5 God is in the midst of her: she shal not be moued; God shall helpe her, and that right early.

6 The heathen raged, the kingdomes were moued: he vttered his voyce, the earth melted.

7 The LORD of hosts is with vs; the God of Iacob is our refuge. Selah.

8 Come, behold the workes of the LORD, what desolations hee hath made in the earth.

9 He maketh warres to cease vnto the end of the earth: hee breaketh the bow, and cutteth the speare in sunder, he burneth the chariot in the fire.

10 Be stil, and know that I am God: I will bee exalted among the heathen, I will be exalted in the earth.

11 The LORD of hosts is with vs; the God of Iacob is our refuge. *Selah*

Those Lingering Pronouns for God

As you can see, the Elizabethan English is easy to understand in the above passage. It is, after all, modern English, at least by linguistic standards. The spelling differs only slightly. The thing that jumps out the most is the print for a *u* looks like a *v*, and vice versa, because these letters were interchangeable at the time. Verse 10 is interesting in that *be* is spelled with one *e* at the beginning and then spelled *bee* a few words down. This is a great example of how spelling had not become completely standardized yet. I thought at first this was a misprint (the 1611 version was known for having some misprints which had to be corrected in later printings), but I found *be* spelled both ways throughout the Bible.

When the King James Version was being translated, English was still changing at a fast pace compared to later centuries. The *bee* spelling was probably beginning to give way to *be*, just as the use of *thee, thou, ye,* and *you* were also already giving way to just plain *you. You,* as we have discussed in an earlier chapter, was always in use, but only as part of that quartet of second-person pronouns. Then *you* just sort of took over for the other three as English continued to simplify. Because the King James Bible was, for the most part, the only Bible used by English speaking Protestants for over three centuries, using *thee* and *thou* came to be thought of as a kind of religious language and, to many, the only proper way to speak to God. Long after *thee's* and *thou's* had completely disappeared from common speech, children as well as adults were still expected to use them in their prayers as a form of respect to God. Even until around 1960 or so, most pastors still used these long-outdated pronouns when praying before their congregations.

There's one real bit of irony in the history behind this lingering religious talk. As these archaic pronouns began dying out in Elizabethan society, they first became relegated for use with those lower in station than oneself, whereas the new, broader use of *you* was reserved for those of equal or greater social standing. In contrast, however, the *thee's* and *thou's* were preserved by later Christians (who had never really used those words in everyday language) in the exact opposite way—reserving the *thee's* and *thou's* for God!

In the original Greek and Hebrew there was never any special language used when addressing God. Prayers were made using the exact same pronouns for God as for everyone else. When the King James Bible was first translated, it reflected this perfectly. But English is alive and just wouldn't hold still. The language changed but the KJV froze this Elizabethan word usage into our religious language for quite a while—over 300 years.

The Legacy

In the chapter on Tyndale, we examined several aspects of his choices in translating that went into making his work so memorable. Not only was the King James Bible based on all of Tyndale's work, but also the scholars who penned this classic translation were a perfect extension of Tyndale's sense of style, clarity, and love for pure, short Anglo-Saxon words. Their focus on accuracy, along with a keen sensitivity for cadence and rhythm of speech, culminated in a work of literature that remains unrivaled.

The biblical scholars of our day possess a greater number of Greek manuscripts, some of which are of more ancient origin than those that were available to the King James translators. Our modern Bible translations make use of these documents, and yet today's scholars agree that there are no serious errors of any kind in the King James translation. Considering their primary focus, the King James translators were in sync with the most savvy of modern scholars, for their goal was the same as ours—produce the most accurate Bible possible and produce it in everyday speech.

The chief thing that singles out the King James Bible from all others is that no other Bible has had, or ever will have, the same kind of impact on our language. The King James Bible was produced at the perfect moment in history for it to make a deep and indelible impression on our English tongue. First, it was produced at the beginning of the modern English period. If it had been produced much earlier, it would have been written in Middle English and not so easily read today. It would now just be another old interesting tome to be dusted off and studied in English classes along with Chaucer. Secondly, the King James Bible came out while the English language was still fluid and malleable, before the great deluge of grammar books, dictionaries, and dogmatic rulings on the right and wrong way to say things. That ominous (and, admittedly, somewhat necessary) onslaught of grammar police and their wily rules did not hit until the late 1700's. But back in 1611, English was like a soft, moist, unbaked dough, and the King James Bible helped knead and shape it into the kind of language that could truly feed the multitudes. As Allister McGrath says in his book on the making of the King James Bible:

> It can be argued that, until the end of the First World War, the King James Bible was seen, not simply as the most important English translation of the Bible, but as one of the finest literary works in the English language. It did not follow literary trends; it established them.

The Man Behind the Team

The King James Version of the Bible should always be viewed as a team effort to finish the product of one man's work, and that one man, without a doubt, is William Tyndale. More than anyone else, he is responsible for the legacy of the English Bible. He alone was a genuine pioneer carving out a whole new territory for the English language, literally taking English where it had never gone before. Tyndale stretched and pulled our language into new shapes, and after he was through, the ability of English to express the deepest truths of God and the most poetic thoughts of man was never questioned again. He had the passion and the genius that gave us God's word in the language of our hearts, a calling for which he was willing to die. He, most of all, should not be forgotten.

Translation it is that openeth the window to let in the light;
that breaketh the shell that we may eat the kernel.

Preface, Holy Bible, King James Version 1611

Part VI

Shakespeare and Modern English

From 1500 Onward

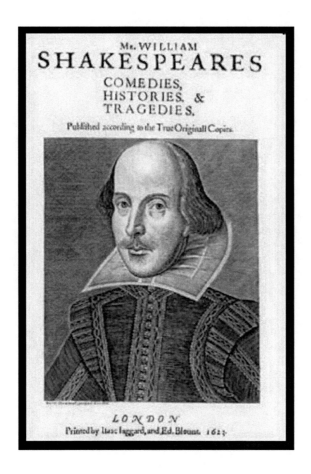

The surprising thing to most people is that
Shakespeare is *modern* English.
(Are they absolutely certain about that?)

Shakespeare

Chapter 14

All the world's a stage,
And all the men and women merely players;
They have their exits and their entrances,
And one man in his time plays many parts...

From *As You Like It*,
William Shakespeare

A Class By Himself

There is no better introduction to William Shakespeare than Professor Elliot Engel's in his entertaining audio lecture entitled "How William Became Shakespeare."

> When you talk about Shakespeare, you are talking about someone who enjoys a reputation that is different from every other human being who has ever picked up a pen and written in any country at any time. There is everybody else who writes, and then there is William Shakespeare. That cannot be said about any other writer that we study either in the history of the English language or in any other.

Professor Engel goes on to say that you will never see Shakespeare's name on a list of the "top ten writers in English," or the "five best authors in the English language," because Shakespeare is simply, and always, in a class by himself. He is never one of the best. He is *the* best. Period. And not only that, some even claim that Shakespeare is the greatest writer of all time in *any* language.

Shakespeare's Inventions

By Shakespeare's day English had finally reached complete respectability, but it had not yet become bound up in the trappings of too many grammar rules or spelling rules or much of any rules, for that matter. In *The Story of English,* the authors describe the remarkable freedom of Elizabethan English:

> Almost any word could be used in almost any part of speech. Adverbs could be used for verbs, nouns for adjectives; nouns and adjectives could take the place of verbs and adverbs. In Elizabethan English you could happy your friend, malice or foot your enemy, or fall an axe on his neck.

No one used this freewheeling English more boldly and creatively than William Shakespeare. And not only did he use words creatively, he also used an enormous amount of words. Researchers have found that Shakespeare employed an amazing 20,138 words in his works. (To give you an idea of how many that is, the King James Bible used a vocabulary of around just 8,000.) And of those 20,000 or so words, at least 1,700 were his own invention. A small sampling of the words Shakespeare spawned:

amazement	exposure	lonely
bedroom	fitful	road
bump	frugal	radiance
courtship	generous	sneak
critic	gloomy	submerge
dwindle	gnarled	useless
eventful	hurry	

Besides new words, Shakespeare invented new phrases. His phrases have become so much a part of our daily speech that the story is often told of a high school student being forced to attend one of Shakespeare's plays and afterwards complaining that it was too full of overused expressions and clichés! Of course, when Shakespeare wrote these expressions, they were all brand new and fresh from his incomparable mind. Here are just a few:

civil tongue	eye sore
cold comfort	fancy free

foregone conclusion	all that glitters is not gold
laughing stock	won't budge an inch
love affair	be that as it may
snow white	as luck would have it
tongue-tied	be-all and end-all
one fell swoop	dead as a door-nail
in a pickle	more sinned against than sinning
it's Greek to me	what's done is done
forever and a day	your own flesh and blood
heart of gold	the milk of human kindness
the more the merrier	

William Shakespeare had a monumental impact on our language. In fact, he was a kind of mini-invasion of the English language all by himself.

Along with his influence upon our vocabulary and turns of phrase, Shakespeare remains unparalleled in two other important aspects of his writing: (1) The extent of his overall knowledge, and (2) His insight into human motivation.

The Extent of His Knowledge

Shakespeare's plays demonstrate a vast array of knowledge of a truly enormous range of subjects. It is so vast, in fact, that it became the basis for various arguments (some of which still float around out there on the Internet) that Shakespeare was not the true author of the works ascribed to him. The argument basically goes like this: It is not possible that one man could have had the span of knowledge that is reflected in the plays ascribed to William Shakespeare. His plays show an understanding of botany, astronomy, law, medicine, geography, history, politics and literature to the extent that no one person could have written them, and certainly not a country boy who just made it through grammar school. Instead, it must have been a team of men who wrote them.

Though at times this argument has drawn attention from various scholars, mainstream thinking stands behind Shakespeare as being the author of the plays ascribed to him. However, the argument certainly serves as a powerful testimony to Shakespeare's genius. It also testifies to the surprising quality of Shakespeare's grammar school and the solid educational background it provided.

Elizabethan grammar schools were more rigorous than our own and the one Shakespeare attended was one of the best in his day. He went to the King Edward IV grammar school in Stratford on Avon (on the Avon River), a rural town not too far from London and the place where he grew up. English grammar schools of this period trained boys beginning at age seven through age fourteen. The boys were kept busy with classical studies for eleven hours each day of summer, nine hours in winter (due to decreasing daylight), for five-and-a-half days each week, and forty or more weeks each year. This amounted to almost double the amount of time a modern child is in class (not a happy thought, is it?). Couple this education with a brilliant mind, a razor-sharp memory, and a natural curiosity so that education continues well beyond the school years and you get...well, Shakespeare!

His Insight

Up until the modern era, teachers wanted to ground their students not only in good literature, but also in literature that encouraged good moral behavior (what a concept). Shakespeare gave educators the best of both, great literature from a thoroughly moral base, and that's one reason teachers have been making their students study Shakespeare for the last 400 years. His themes, his characters, and his plots all emerge from an overall Christian worldview.

However, though Shakespeare writes from a Christian point of view, he is never simplistic. Like the Bible itself, which does not gloss over the sinfulness of even its finest heroes (such as David who committed both adultery and murder), Shakespeare draws us into the lives of full and complex heroes and villains. We may pity the villain or see fatal flaws in the hero. Sometimes we identify with both. Shakespeare hides wisdom in the mouth of his fools at times, and a wise king may do very foolish things. He uses his characters to illustrate that life may become absurd and fruitless, but it is usually *after* that character has fallen to the "dark side."

For instance, Macbeth speaks a very well known and often quoted soliloquy on the utter meaninglessness of life:

> To-morrow, and to-morrow, and to-morrow,
> Creeps in this petty pace from day to day,
> To the last syllable of recorded time;
> And all our yesterdays have lighted fools

The way to dusty death. Out, out, brief candle!
Life's but a walking shadow, a poor player,
That struts and frets his hour upon the stage,
And then is heard no more. It is a tale
Told by an idiot, full of sound and fury,
Signifying nothing.

Macbeth Act 5, scene 5

The view of life expressed here certainly does not sound biblical. However, Macbeth reaches these powerfully haunting conclusions only *after* he has committed a heinous crime. Macbeth's willful act of murder has ushered his soul into a very dark place indeed, and his actions have distorted his thinking and his perceptions about life. Paul describes a similar process in Romans chapter 1 where he says wicked behavior leads to a darkened mind.

In the end, if you look at "the long and short of it" (to quote Shakespeare), Shakespeare consistently illustrates throughout all his works that sin leads to suffering and that life is imbued with purpose and meaning only when a person strives for what is right, honest, and good. Most Christians of the eighteenth and nineteenth centuries felt the two key books for any educated person to own were the King James Bible and the Complete Works of William Shakespeare. Is it any wonder?

There are many books on Shakespeare, his life, the period of history during which he lived, and the early theaters of London, especially the Globe Theater with which Shakespeare is most often identified. So read all you can about Shakespeare. But most of all, read Shakespeare. Watch the movies that have been produced from his plays. Go to his plays! No other medium brings Shakespeare's works to life better than a troupe of players in live action before a responding audience. He was a playwright not a novelist; his works were meant to be *performed*. After all, and to quote Shakespeare again, "The play's the thing."

✠✠✠ ℭℰ ✠✠✠

Love is not love

Which alters when it alteration finds

Or bends with the remover to remove.

O, no, it is an ever-fixèd mark

That looks on tempests and is never shaken...

From Sonnet 116

"I had rather hear my dog bark at a crow than a man swear he loves me."

Beatrice (who, of course, falls in love),

Act I, Scene I, Much Ado About Nothing

"The first thing we do, let's kill all the lawyers."

Act IV, Scene II, King Henry the Sixth, Part II

More than 80 spelling variations are recorded for Shakespeare's name, from Shappere to Shaxberd. In the few signatures that have survived, Shakespeare signed his name Willm Shaksp, William Shakespe, Wm Shakspe, William Shakspere, Willm Shakspere, and William Shakspeare. He never once spelled it as we do today— Shakespeare.

If Only King Alfred Could See Us Now!

Chapter 15

They have been at a great feast of languages,
and have stolen the scraps.

William Shakespeare

So, what's been happening to English since Shakespeare's day? Well...why don't you tell me? You know enough now to make at least some basic assumptions. First, you've learned one key feature of all living languages—they are changing. No grammar book and no dictionary can halt the metamorphosis of a language. If a language is being spoken, it's moving along with the people who speak it, with the culture in which it is embedded. Along with that principle, you probably remember the number one law about language change: *Living languages always simplify over time.* Thus, you could tell me with the confidence of a true linguist that (1) English has surely continued to change, and (2) it has become simplified in its grammar. You would be exactly right. However, even though the grammar itself has become more streamlined, the rules for using the grammar have become more numerous and exact.

The Genesis of Grammar Rules

At the time of the publication of the King James Bible and the plays of William Shakespeare, English had finally begun to achieve literary status among the educated and scholarly of society, and soon English linguistics was a serious field of study. Scholars began tackling English to understand and describe its rules of operation. They also began describing finer points of how educated speakers speak and learned writers write. People began studying these descriptions so they could sound educated too. Having some guidelines to follow gives an author assurance that he is writing in the way most acceptable to the largest number of readers. Dictionaries were written, grammar books were composed, and schools began to adopt specific guidelines for spelling and grammar. The guidelines began as *descriptions* of how we speak and write, but they morphed into *standards*. The idea of a "right" way and a "wrong" way to speak and write emerged, and the standards became more frozen.

Despite this process of being analyzed and codified, the language along with its rules continued to change. Thus, some of what's considered incorrect or correct in the twenty-first century may have been deemed just the opposite in the past. Some changes came along in spite of the new movement toward fixed standards, and some came along because of it.

I Ain't Going to Use No Double Negatives

Both the use of *ain't* and the use of the double negative are good examples of shifting grammar standards. There was once a perfectly respectable use for *ain't*. Jane Austen, the famous 18th century British author, used it. "Ain't I" was short for "am I not?" or, more accurately, "am not I?" as in, "I'm beautiful, ain't I?" *Ain't* was the contraction for *am not*. So, what happened to it? Why can't we use *ain't* now? Today, the correct form is to say, "Aren't I?" which put straightforward would be "I are not," and that sure isn't grammatically correct! Shakespeare also used *ain't*. He used double negatives, too. But that's not never permitted by no English teacher today. So what happened? For *ain't*, it became a matter of class distinction. *Ain't* was used incorrectly so often by the less well-educated members of society that gradually educated people abandoned even the correct use of it. Before long, grammar books declared it incorrect. In the case of the double negative, grammarians decided that two negatives logically contradicted each other and thus were "incorrect." Never mind that writers from Chaucer to Shakespeare had used the double negative effectively for centuries to add emphasis.

That or Which?

Another example of grammar rules springing from the influence of overly anxious grammarians is the case of *that* and *which*. Have you ever been composing something on your computer and found that Microsoft Word underscored an error saying you need to replace *that* with *which*, or vice versa? Well, Francis and Henry Fowler invented the rule for the "proper" use of *that* and *which* in 1906. They simply didn't like the random way these two words operated and decided there should be a formula to govern which word to use when. They constructed a rule that sounded logical and put it into their best-selling grammar text, *The King's English*. They designated *which* for use with non-restrictive clauses, and they pronounced *that* to be better suited to restrictive clauses. Many perfectly good writers have never gone by this rule, yet the rule has become so embedded in the textbooks and teacher credos of our day that now even our computers flag it!

A Few Predictions

If the grammar of a language is always changing and simplifying, then it would be a good guess that in a few hundred years some of the rules we follow today will be considered archaic. Perhaps some pronoun cases will have simplified and disappeared along with other shifts in usage. Some linguistic soothsayers predict changes such as these: *shall* shall vanish, *whom* may bite the dust, and the verb inflections for subjunctive mood, which are already on a linguistic resuscitator, will succumb. (Do you even know what the subjunctive mood is?) It has already become acceptable in some circles to end a sentence with a preposition or to split an infinitive, especially if rewording causes the sentence to sound too stilted and formal. Some of these conventions may be entirely forgotten in another few decades.

But before you abandon any of these perfectly proper forms, remember it takes centuries for changes that are mistakes today to reach the high plateau of blessed acceptability. Regardless of how English is changing, learning and using today's good grammar is an essential element of education. The ability to write and speak effectively, of which good grammar is a part, will equip you, *free you*, to communicate your ideas confidently with people from all walks of life. Remember the deck of cards? The cards are the vocabulary; the rules of the game are the grammar. The rules create the game and enable you to play, that is, to communicate. Knowing them well allows you to play at any level.

The Largest Dictionary in the World

When English arrived in England, it was a lean, trim, meaty stock of Anglo-Saxon words. Then over the centuries it feasted on Latin and Norse, gorged on French, and chased down the whole meal with a fizzy swig of Greek and a fresh twist of Latin during the Renaissance. By this time English had greatly expanded its voracious vocabulary, despite the fact that it had also dropped many of its original Anglo-Saxon words.

However, at the close of the Renaissance and around the time of Shakespeare, English vocabulary was still not nearly so vast as it is today. Look at these modern statistics again:

> French dictionary – 100,000 word entries
> Russian dictionary– 130,000
> German dictionary – 185,000 word entries
> Oxford English Dictionary – 615,000 word entries

The English dictionary today is more than triple that of German, the next largest language. In fact, English has the largest stockpile of words of any language anywhere at any time in history. But this didn't just happen overnight. It took global influences and technological infusions occurring over the next few centuries to cultivate this extraordinary growth.

The British Empire

We who live in the 21st century often do not realize just how truly massive was this English colonial conglomerate known as the British Empire. It was not called an empire for nothing. Around 1600, Britain started taking control of lands all over the world. At one time she oversaw colonies on every continent, ruling large swaths of territory in Africa, India, Asia, the Pacific islands, Australia, and North America (until that fateful year of 1776). The British Empire encompassed so much of our globe that Englishmen enjoyed bragging that "the sun never sets on the British Empire."

So now, picture every single harbor into which the British navy sailed not only overflowing with exotic trade goods for sale, but also teeming with exotic new words for the sailors to pick up and take back to England. Every port gushed with foreign words and phrases as juicy as the new tropical fruits. Sailors adopted them—sometimes for fun, sometimes for lack of anything else to call a new thing, and sometimes to sound savvy and sophisticated. There's just nothing like a foreign word bandied about as if you use it all the time to make one sound experienced, well traveled, and knowledgeable. And that went, too, for the thousands of British settlers who came to these lands to help administer, rule, legislate, or just labor and live in the thriving British colonies. So, foreign words were adopted by the boatload, and these verbal stowaways cruised freely from port to port on the lips and in the ears of English speakers all over the globe.

Here's a small sampling just from India alone, a country under British influence or rule for 300 years:

shampoo	cot	veranda
pajamas	loot	calico
bandana	jungle	coolie
bungalow	guru	khaki

English – American Style

After the English language set sail for America and began to dock along the coasts of the New World, it immediately started adopting bits and pieces from the many Native American languages. Algonquin, Iroquois, Cherokee, and Muskogee are among the many tongues that left their indelible rhythm and beauty on the names of our rivers, hills, towns and valleys. Just in my own state of Georgia, we raft down the *Chattahoochee* River, pan for gold in *Dahlonega* (Cherokee for yellow rock), hike the trails of the *Appalachian* Mountains, and visit the Civil War battlefield at *Chickamauga*. But the influence goes way beyond place names. Frontier Americans readily took up such words as: *savanna, skunk, hickory, barbecue, raccoon, scuppernong and squash*. And, of course, there are all those things we still associate with the natives of our country: *moccasin, tomahawk, pow-wow,* and *kayak*, etc. Twenty-six states sport Native American names. The political term *caucus* comes from the Algonquin natives, hinting at the influence Native American tribal government had upon the thinking of some of our most influential founding fathers.

As English developed on the shores of America, the vocabularies of Britain and America began to diverge. Anyone who has traveled in England notices these entertaining differences. In Britain you take a *lift*, not an *elevator*; you don't *line up*, you *queue up*; you get water from a *tap*, not a *faucet*; your car runs on *petrol*, not *gas*; and you make a call on your *mobile*, not a *cell phone*.

Interestingly, sometimes the American version is the one closer to the way Shakespeare would have said it. It is the British who changed in some instances, while we stayed the same. Americans often use the word *fall* for *autumn*. They don't use that much in England now, though once it was common there. Likewise for saying *trash* instead of *rubbish*, and using *loan* as a verb instead of *lend*. All of these "Americanisms" are really older British forms that hearken back to Shakespeare's day, while the British themselves have lost them.

New Words for a New Age

Making up new words out of the blue is not a modern phenomenon, but no other era compares to our own for the staggering number of new words generated in order to name our discoveries and inventions. For every never-before-seen contraption, every discovery of science, every innovative improvement in our lifestyle, and every fresh-out-of-the-imagination new way to do anything, we needed a new word. From airplanes to ballpoint pens, telephones to deodorant, nuclear fusion to panty hose, just think of all that has come along since 1600. We have had a revolution in our living standard. Up until around 1800, most people lived pretty much the way their parents and grandparents lived. Not any more. The biggest change in our era is in change itself—it's happening exponentially faster than at any other time throughout the history of man. And most of the changes have demanded new words.

The explosion in technology has caused the biggest explosion in words. *Electricity, telegraph, quasar, radio, microwave*—we have made up neologisms by the gazillion (a contrived word itself) since technology took off. Just since computer monitors began glowing in everyone's houses, we have witnessed the birth of *byte, gigabyte, hard drive, google* (which quickly morphed from the name of an Internet search engine to a verb), *website, Internet, microchip, download, upload, laptop, floppy disk, flash drive, e-zine, blog*, etc., etc., etc., ad infinitum—literally—because we will certainly go on forever inventing new words for all our wonderful discoveries and technological tools and toys. Today, industry and technology are by far the two strongest stimulants for the creation of words.

But, still, you may be thinking, the French have all this new stuff, too. Why isn't their dictionary just as big? I'm so glad you asked.

Outlawing E-mail

The French have an interesting policy about their language. It is rather mind-boggling that any country would attempt to have a policy about their language, to control it, that is. Language is just so extraordinarily fluid, hard to grasp, impossible to legislate. But the French are giving it a try. The French want to keep their language "pure." They don't want foreign words seeping in. They think that might dilute the Frenchiness of French, so to speak. They love their language and rightly so. It is one of the world's most beautiful languages. So, they don't want it infused with a lot of English words, or Anglicisms, as they call them. They actually have a government commission that studies all new words coming into the French scene, and they make laws about what to call new things. Honest.

For example, according to author Paul Greenberg, they don't want French people to use the term *e-mail*. That sounds too English, too American. They want the French to call it *courriel*. All French government agencies are required to use the word *courriel* and never *e-mail* in their documents or on their websites, and if you're a good citizen you're supposed to follow suit. Another example is the term that Sony coined for an mp3 player: the *Walkman*. The French government wishes it to be called *un baladeur*. Good luck. Thus, you can see how government policy is attempting to keep the French dictionary unpolluted, and that tends also to keep it small.

Liberté Pour Les Mots! (Liberty for Words!)

Meanwhile, America holds out the torch of the Statue of Liberty to welcome immigrant words from all over the globe. We say, "Come as you are. We'll take you in." Below is just a *wee* (Scottish for very small) sampling of the immigrant scalawags in your dictionary:

trek—South African	*boomerang*—Australian
tattoo—Tahitian	*mammoth*—Russian
polo—Tibetan	*boondocks*—Philippines
bazaar—Persian	*ketchup*—Malaysian

typhoon—Chinese	*amen*— Hebrew
opera—Italian	*oasis*—Egyptian
tycoon—Japanese	*potato*—Quechuan
sauna—Finnish	*bungalow*—Bengali
smorgasbord—Swedish	*hurricane*—Caribbean
robot—Czech	*mishmash*—Yiddish
taboo—Tongan	*gung-ho*—Mandarin Chinese
golf—Scots	*cannibal*—Spanish
ukulele—Hawaiian	*jazz*—West African

Linguists estimate that as much as seventy to seventy-five percent of our English vocabulary is foreign.

Mr. Crapper

The origins of most English words have today been fairly well traced, but funny arguments occasionally arise over where a particular word came from. One such squabble is attached to the career of an English plumber in the late 1800's. He was connected with making improvements on the toilet and thereby got his name linked to this marvelous invention that none of us could do without. His name was Mr. Crapper.

Mr. Crapper had a very successful plumbing business in London repairing, servicing, and selling toilets. These early models of the modern toilet had a water tank that hung on the wall above the seat, and Mr. Crapper's toilets had the name CRAPPER spelled out in large letters on the tank as advertisement for his business. And so it was that it became slang among boys in the early 1900's to refer to a bathroom as *the crapper*, though the term was considered too crude to be spoken in polite company. Now the connection between Mr. Crapper's name, calling a bathroom *the crapper*, and the word *crap* seems obvious. Many people drew the logical conclusion that the word *crap* came from Mr. Crapper's name.

However, some historians contend that the best evidence indicates *crap* is actually a much older term and goes back to an early 1400's word that simply meant dirt or waste. From thence the ill-fated word took a downward dive and came to mean more specifically the waste from a person's body. Thus, *crap*, once a decent word for dirt, became a vulgarism, a crude and offensive expression. According to these historians, it was just a coincidence that a Mr. Crapper went into the one profession that would cause mischief among word origin buffs.

The word *dirt*, by the way, is from the Old Norse, and it once meant excrement. So dirt meant crap and crap meant dirt. They switched places.

How Words Morph and Mutate

As illustrated above, words have careers all their own. They can move up, down, and sideways in social standing. We've seen how they sometimes even switch places. Linguists toss word-changes into particular categories. Here are some of them—

Upward climb: A *steward* used to be a lowly pig keeper. The word moved up in the world and now means a custodian or supervisor, someone with more important responsibilities.

Downward Dive: *Villain* once meant someone who owned a villa (house), then it slowly slithered down to its sinister meaning today. The word *crap*, discussed above, is another example of the dive.

Sideways Shift (changes that do not shift the negative or positive valence of a word): *Clerk* once referred to a clergyman. Then, because clergymen were the only ones who could read and write in the Middle Ages, the word logically shifted to mean anyone who could keep records and manage business affairs, someone more like a secretary, and that's how we use it today.

Concrete to Abstract: *Dreary* once meant something concrete (a thing as opposed to an idea). A dreary was anything that was dripping or covered with blood. Over time, its meaning shifted toward the abstract and it morphed into an adjective that meant horrid. Then, losing even more of its intensity, it became our modern synonym for dull and gloomy.

Abstract to Concrete: *Biddan* began as an abstract concept during the early Middle Ages. It meant asking or praying. When Roman Catholics prayed, they often used (and still do) what's known as a rosary, a string of polished stones or small wooden balls that stood for specific prayers, or biddans, to be recited. Eventually, the stones themselves came to be called biddans, which in turn shape-shifted into our concrete, modern word *bead*.

The Biggest Language Invasion of All: English Invades the World

When King Alfred came to the throne, England was a small king-dom on a relatively unimportant island. He struggled to unite the English people by promoting their common language. At the time, it must have seemed a grand hope just to make English respectable in that one spot on the globe. No doubt, he would have trouble comprehending the amazing world status of his native tongue today. English has grown from being the one invaded into being itself the biggest invader of all. English is the official or first language in forty-five countries and is now spoken by around 350 million people. It is the preferred second language of millions more. Richard Lederer writes:

> The majority of the world's books, newspapers, and magazines are written in English. Most interna-tional telephone calls are made in English. Sixty percent of the world's radio programs are beamed in English, and more than seventy percent of international mail and seventy-five percent of cable messages and telexes are written and addressed in English. It is the language in which two thirds of all scientific treatises and technical periodicals are printed and eighty percent of all com-puter text stored.
>
> *The Miracle of Language*

Throughout the Middle Ages and beyond, Latin was considered an international language, but Latin was only used by scholars, and only those particular scholars who lived in Europe. In contrast, English is a truly global language, and it is for *everyone*. What a rich heritage we possess! We speak and write and think in the language of men such as Bede, Chaucer, Tyndale, Shakespeare, and, of course, King Alfred.

Alfred's humble hope was merely to give English a bit of an edge over Latin, to make it respectable in educated circles. He was happy to see English in handwritten books being carried on foot from monastery to monastery. How amazed would he be at the triumph of English today? English zings through the air on TV and radio waves, in emails and IM's, through cell phones and blackberries. It spins and crawls in webbots and search engines over a worldwide web that connects the synapses of the world. The plain and common tongue of English now extends all over the globe.

Writing for the Associated Press in 2009, Ted Anthony remarked, "When Pope John Paul II arrived in the Middle East last month to retrace Christ's footsteps and addressed Christians, Muslims and Jews, the pontiff spoke not Latin, not Arabic, not Hebrew, not his native Polish. He spoke in English."

If only King Alfred could see us now!

⁜⁜⁜ Æ ⁜⁜⁜

To be brief, I may say that it has ever been my desire to live honorably while I was alive, and after my death, to leave to them that should come after me my memory in good works.

King Alfred

Resources

The Anglo-Saxon Chronicle, translated and collated by Anne Savage. Published by CLB International, Godalming, Surrey, 1997. Actually fun to browse and very quirky in spots, such as the entry about folks seeing dragons. (Available free online)

Austen, Jane. *The History of England.* Introduction by A.S. Byatt with a note on the text by Deirdre Le Faye. Algonquin Books of Chapel Hill, Chapel Hill, North Carolina, 1993. Jane Austen wrote this whimsical mini-history when she was sixteen introducing herself with the words: "By a partial, prejudiced, & ignorant Historian," and she notes later, "There will be very few Dates in this History."

Bobrick, Benson. *Wide as the Waters, The Story of the English Bible and The Revolution It Inspired.* Simon and Schuster, New York, New York, 2001. A rich, in-depth look at the people, politics and events that led up to the King James Version of the Bible and beyond.

Childress, Diana. *Chaucer's England.* Linnet Books, North Haven, Connecticut, 2000. A wonderful text! Great for middle school and above. It fleshes out the era of Chaucer from the impact of the Black Plague to the political scene.

Churchill, Winston. *Birth of Britain.* This is the first volume of Churchill's four-volume tome, *A History of the English Speaking Peoples.* It is available for just $5 as an e-book through Barnes and Noble.

Daniell, David. *William Tyndale, A Biography.* Yale University Press, 1994. Daniell is a University of London scholar and chairman of the William Tyndale Society.

Engel, Eliot. *How William Became Shakespeare.* I became a fan of Professor Engel after hearing him lecture on Robert E. Lee at our local library. I recommend all of his CD's and DVD's. His interesting and enthusiastic lectures never fail to disclose fascinating tidbits about his subjects that are simply not found anywhere else. He's one of a kind. Check him out at <www.authorsink.com>

Everyday Life Through the Ages, edited and designed by The Reader's Digest Association Limited, London, 1992. A richly illustrated guide to the everyday lives of people from all places throughout history, geared toward a seventh grade audience and up. It was right at my level.

Holy Bible, The. King James Version facsimile reproduction of the 1611 first folio edition. Hendrickson Publishers, Oct. 2003.

Lederer, Richard. *The Miracle of Language.* Pocket Books, Simon and Schuster Inc., New York, NY, 1991. This book is entertaining and fun. It is packed full of fascinating information on the English language and on specific authors who have helped shape it.

McCrum, Robert, William Cran, and Robert MacNeil. *The Story of English.* Viking Penguin, Inc. New York, 1986. The amazing tome upon which the PBS special of the same name was based.

McDowell, Josh. *The New Evidence That Demands A Verdict.* Revised updated edition, Thomas Nelson, 1999. McDowell covers evidence for accuracy of the biblical record as well as the claims of Christ. An excellent resource.

McGrath, Alister. *In The Beginning.* Anchor Books, division of Random House, Inc., New York, 2001. A comprehensive study on the King James Bible, how it came to be, and its impact on our faith and language.

Norton Anthology of English Literature, Revised, Vol. I. W. W. Norton and Co., 1968.

Williams, Joseph M. *Style, Ten Lessons in Clarity and Grace.* Fifth Addition. Addison-Wesley Educational Publisher Inc., 1997. This is the best book I've ever seen on how to write clearly and effectively. It is concise and easy to read but so dense with good advice one needs to read it again and again.

Internet Sites

"Bede's World." Online site for the Museum of Medieval Northumbria at Jarrow, a museum dedicated to the Venerable Bede. < http://www.bedesworld.co.uk/academic-bede.php >

Bible Gateway. Read the King James Version or any of several modern ones here, including the Douay Rheims and Wycliffe New Testament. Also there is a full Greek and Hebrew Bible reference section here. < www.Biblegateway.com/versions>

The British Library Online. Go to the "Learning Area" for interactive student activities and much, much more. <www.bl.uk>

British Broadcasting Company Interactive History. Great site developed by
the BBC for teachers and students. It has incredible online educational games and other aids.
<www.bbc.co.uk/history/timelines/britain>

Bosworth and Toller. The University of Pennsylvania's complete Anglo-
Saxon dictionary.
<www.ling.upenn.edu/~kurisuto/germanic/oe_bosworthtoller_ab
out.html>

Children of the Code. A website on alphabets, spelling, writing, and the
history of the efforts toward spelling reforms.
<www.childrenofthecode.org/code-history/index.htm>

The Canterbury Tales and Other Works. For all things Middle English—has
audio files so you can actually hear the Middle English spoken.
<http://www.librarius.com>

"Changes in Language Since Shakespeare's Time." Details on English shifts
from the 1600's with examples from Shakespeare and the 1611 KJV.
<http://bartleby.com/224/1504.html>

The Complete Works of William Shakespeare. A Shakespeare site operated
by *The Tech,* M.I.T.'s oldest newspaper.
<http://shakespeare.mit.edu/>

Internet Medieval Sourcebook. New York's Fordham University online site
for medieval history and literature.
<http://www.fordham.edu/halsall/sbook1k.html>

King Alfred's Grammar Book. All about Old English—much more than just
grammar.
<http://acunix.wheatonma.edu/mdrout/GrammarBook2005/KAG
rammar.html>

King James Version of the Bible. This is the King James Bible of 1611 but
the spellings have been updated.
<http://etext.virginia.edu/kjv.browse.html>

"Language and Linguistics." National Science Foundation. Hear audio
clips of changes in English.
<www.nsf.gov/news/special_reports/linguistics/paths.jsp>

Luminarium: Anthology of English Literature. Read full texts here plus
articles and essays about individual works of literature along with
excellent summaries of various authors' lives.

"Manuscript Evidence for Superior New Testament Reliability." The chart in chapter 9 comparing the reliability of other ancient manuscripts with the New Testament came from this site. <www.carm.org/questions/about-bible/manuscript-evidence-superior-new-testament-reliability>

Online Etymology Dictionary. A dictionary of word histories. <www.etymonline.com>

Shearer, Rob. *A Walk Through History.* This free, unique audio seminar is a capsule-sized, one-hour overview of western civilization by one of the publishers at Greenleaf Press, a publishing business and supplier of quality books for children and young adults. <http://www.greenleafpress.com>

Tolkien Society Study Pack: Runes. This particular page is on Anglo Saxon runes and the way in which J.R.R. Tolkien, author of The Lord of the Rings Trilogy, made use of runes in his books. Tolkien was an Anglo Saxon scholar and professor at Oxford University and this site is rich and full of much more than just the lesson on runes. <http://www.tolkiensociety.org/ed/study_02.html>

William Tyndale Gallery. This is my favorite site on Tyndale and his work. <http://www.williamtyndale.com/0welcomewilliamtyndale.htm>

For links to videos, articles, images, and literature related to
each chapter of the book, go to the author's website—
www.theshorterword.com

About the Author

Laurie White lives with her husband, Avery, in the middle of the woods in a log house surrounded by maple trees and white-tailed deer that eat her daylilies. Their Covington, Georgia home reflects their mutual interests, from flintlock rifles to refinished furniture and old bookshelves that sag with too many history books. Besides writing fiction and non-fiction for children and young adults, Laurie has taught both English and history in middle school and high school. She is a former homeschooling mom of three children who are now grown.

LaVergne, TN USA
15 April 2010
179338LV00003B/3/P